Captives of the Cosmic Web

The Book of the Painting

by

Bernard Barnes

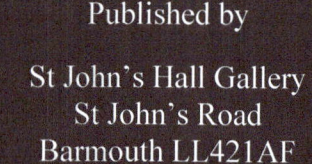

Published by

St John's Hall Gallery
St John's Road
Barmouth LL421AF

Tel: 07767862382

www.bernardbarnes.com

www.stjohnshallgallery.com

Synapticconnections@btopenworld.com

ISBN-13: 978-1515285069

ISBN-10: 1515285065

The Cloud

Paintings inspired by the particulate universe

This book is an introduction to the work of Welsh born artist Bernard Barnes, and in particular the large wall painting 'The Captives of the Cosmic Web'. The panel of 25 canvases are hung on the north wall of St John's Hall Gallery, Barmouth.

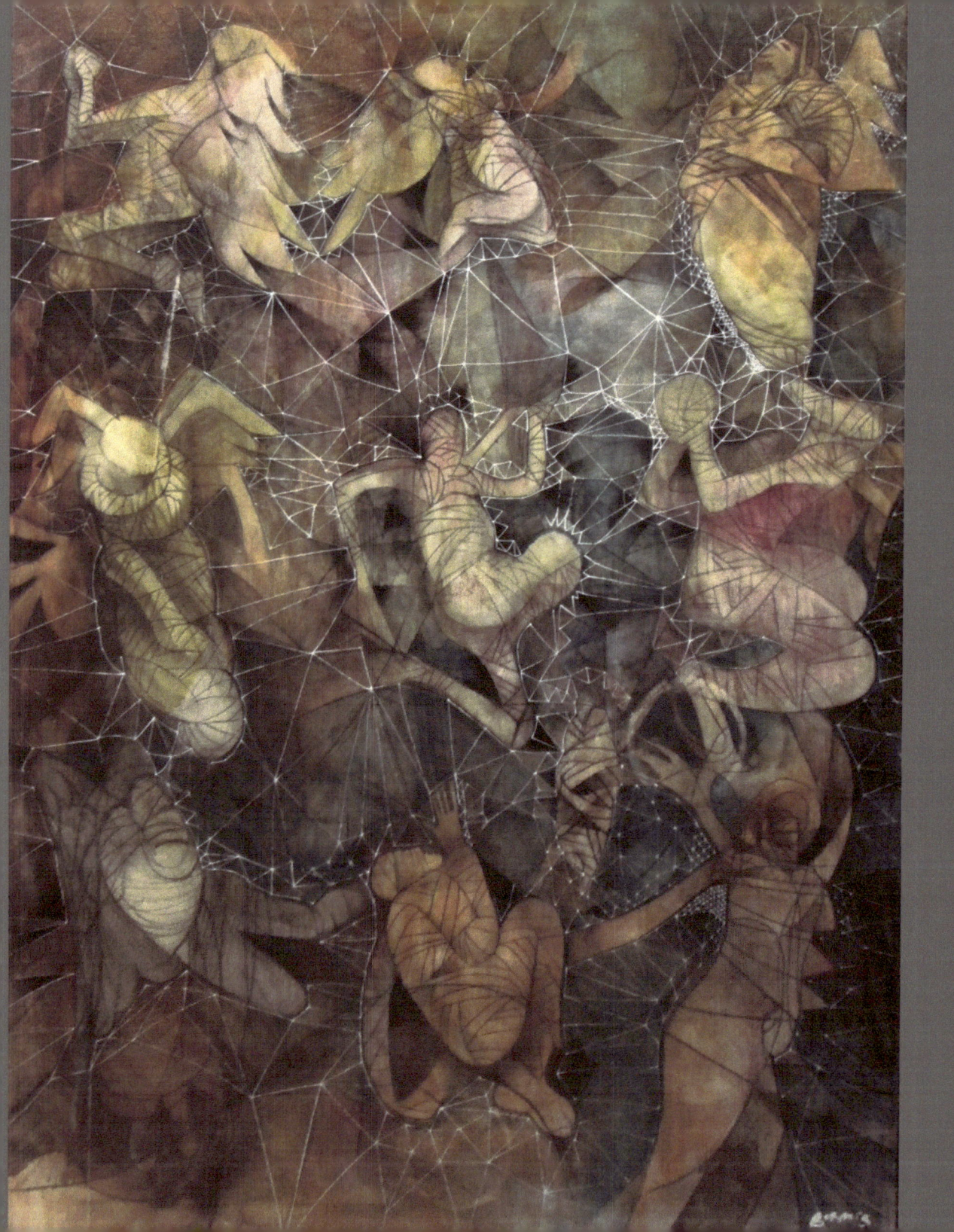

Bound Angels

is an important painting for me. It began a series that ran parallel with discoveries I was making in other area. In particular I became interested in science and the discoveries men were making in all sorts of branches of science, from insect eyes to red giants. A new understanding of the universe was supplanting the old. Our timeless obsession with religion seemed at last to be at an end. Now, after so many achievements, Einstein to Newton, Maxwell, Mendeleev and so on, we discover dark matter.

Being in the dark is the common condition of mankind. That is why I conceive, in my paintings, of the background condition of a picture to be dark, very dark sometimes, and sometimes swirling. The action goes on in a theatrical space in front of this background.

Line is thought, quicksilver movement, connecting point to point, being information. I love line, it is the dominant element to my work. I am fascinated by the way lines can be used to define points and build structure. Space remains space, but by the subtle use of chiaroscuro we may define crystalline mass within. This mass may be modified with tone or colour, it may be crushed here or there, or stretched.

Things may be inserted, embedded, into this mass, so that situations, even narratives, can be formed. It is infinitely adaptable to my needs. It is also the way the universe seems to be constructed.

This small painting led to a series of similar studies. I call them the 'Cloud' series. They are all illustrated in the next few pages. From this series came the idea for the large painting 'The Captives of the Cosmic Web'. That title came later, only after I understood what direction the painting was going towards.

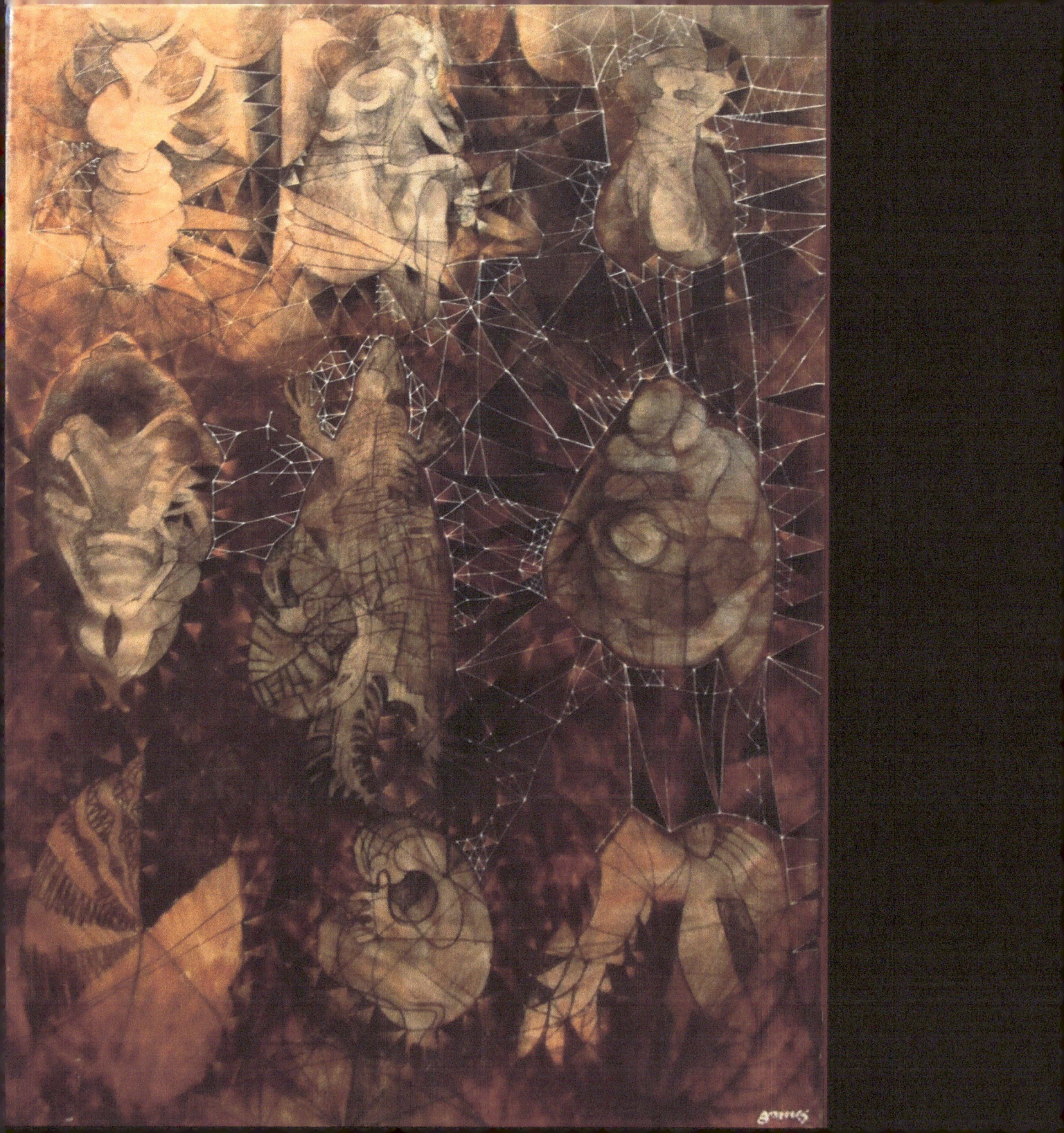

PRIMAL

There is a layer around the earth, a biosphere like an atmosphere. In here is a hugely dynamic region stretching from the high air to the deepest caves. It is inhabited by trillions of living creatures being born, sustaining themselves, and dying. Teeming billions of points of life, of dynamic replicators, of dynamic communicators.

The biosphere is a web of events transmuting energy into form and more and more elaborate form. Energy sheds off these bright burning mobile tenacious dangerous things that are the points of life. They gather, these burning points, in swarms, in flocks, in clouds, in tempests they swim and fly and crawl and slip, they scuttle and burrow and rob and kill. They consume each other, these points of life. Those who eat burn brightest.

These darting, calling, moving, fluttering beings are filled up and are filled by the web with sound and movement. Engaging matter in a gigantic struggle against inevitable inertia, these carapaces are cast off, to hang in the web of the universe. Here is the nursery inside the furnace of the early earth. In the water, bubbling slimy things, crusty things like rock, begin to grow. Creatures shedding the membranes of themselves to become larger, Chrysalises pupate and metamorphose. A swelling, creaking, rattling, carapacious tearing, bony cracking, rhythmic pumping of liquid, squeezing into lace wing like maps and network of vesicles. It is the ancient elemental struggle of creatures within the web of the universe, going on still.

Mountains have risen out of the sea made of these bodies. Temples are carved out of these ancient limestone bodies.

Though the countless lives have ended they are here in form at lease, hanging still in the universe, in the great net of time.

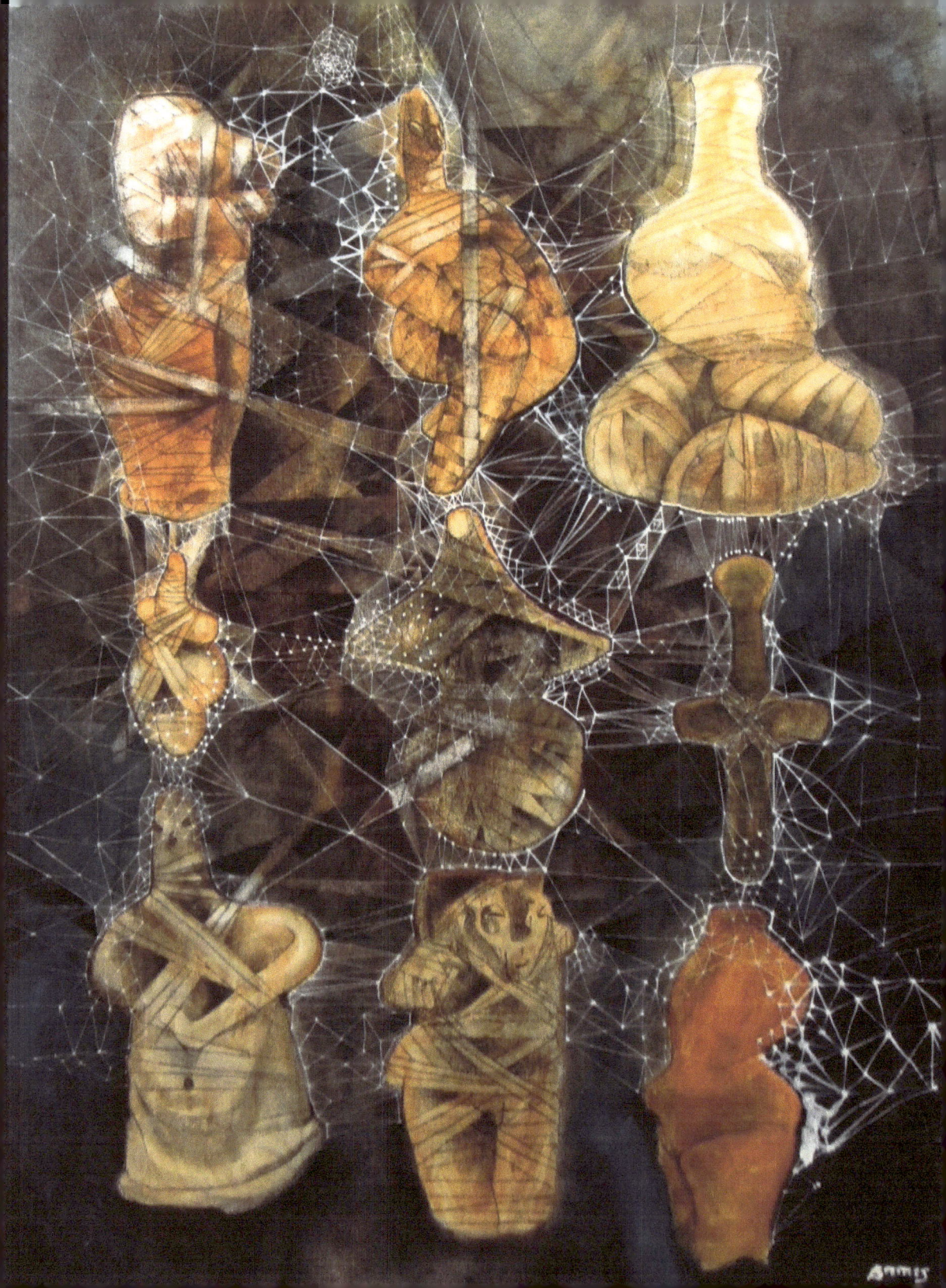

ANCESTORS

Thoughts hang beside the objects in this curious universe. Thoughts have shapes too linking synapse to synapse in the minds, fleeting like music, but not abstract as we think of thought, but actual, composed of dilated blood vessels and activated neurons, fleeting shapes forming in the vast universe of brain cells, flickering with conscious thought. Symbolism has come into being.

There has arisen, in this chaotic universe, an intelligent eye, a curious ear, not just for food, for stalking or avoiding, but for seeing and remembering, enquiring and standing in awe.

The ancestor becomes the deity, the progenitor becomes a knot of thoughts, leading from the minds of a multitude. No single man made these cords. They were woven in the dense web of time.

The clay is formed by thought, into the shape of the mother, the tunnel from which all of life has emerged. It all come from the mother.

They replicated and prosper sometimes. They were defeated by disease and ill fortune; wild enemies imprisoned them and worse, sometimes. And when the bronze warriors were all gone, their arrow tips prized by museums, these mothers still hang in the web, redolent with their old mysteries.

Look at the web they have woven. It is like lace, like tatting spreading out its fans, in patterns, so the primal deities are hung in the great void of our universe.

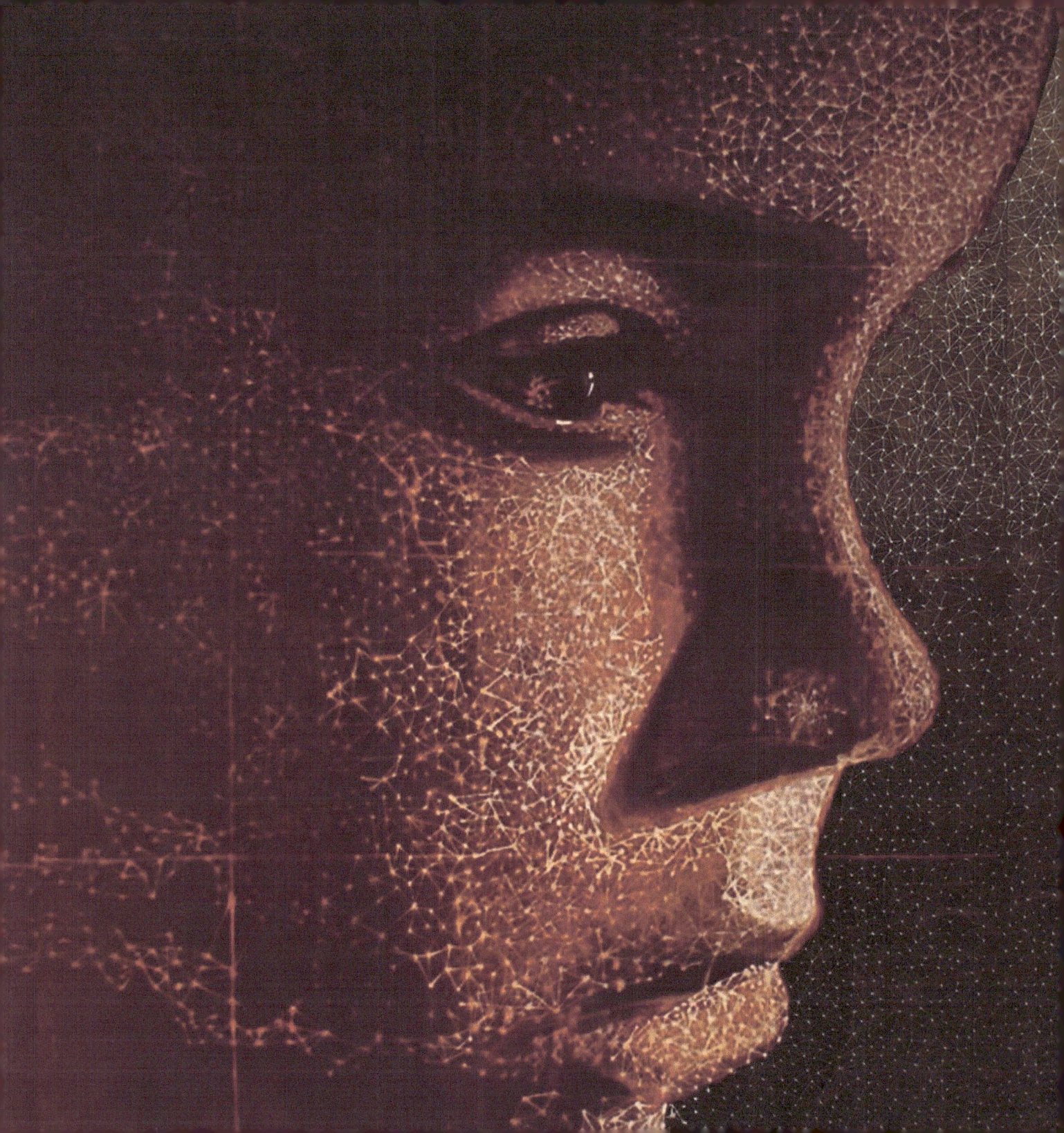

ANCIENT CITIES

So many things have passed. Most are forgotten. Ur of the Chaldees is now a mark in the desert. But it is still a mark. If we had forgotten its name, there would still be a mark. A small thing perhaps, set against the lives that have been lived within its walls.

It transpires that these empty shells, the shells of old cities, still hang in the universe like petrified lace. They are most beautiful to look at, to examine in the large and the detail.

When we examine the dead cities we can see their fragility, more complex by far than the hive or the nest of the other super organisms. Each one of these; (Megiddo is there, Amsterdam too. Luca in Italy at the time of the renaissance), look like the skulls of a strange animals. Certainly they housed and protected the central nervous system of the creature lived within the numerous caverns and pathways of the citadels. Each is a cranium as well as a citadel.

The living creature within made a great noise when it was alive. The city was a reverberant place, full of chambers and hollows, halls and houses. Laugher, cries, shouts, cheers, musicing and dancing, bellowing of animals, screams and trumpeting.

These form carry their own memories implicit in their form; (An early village at the heart of the citadel. A street plan based on a tented encampment for example). A process, a whole culture, lies embedded in these complex shapes. They are inert, but their form has its own meaning, a pattern of great beauty is now woven into the fabric of the universe. Look closely and you can see carvings of all the gods and their interactions with us, gilded sprays of foliage carved in precious stones. The universe sometimes sheds objects of wondrous beauty, and some of these things are still hanging in the web, more enduring than ambergris or the wing decorations on a butterfly.

An ancient city is a pattern, a small area of meaning, with extensions of that meaning merging outwards at the perimeter with the unknown.

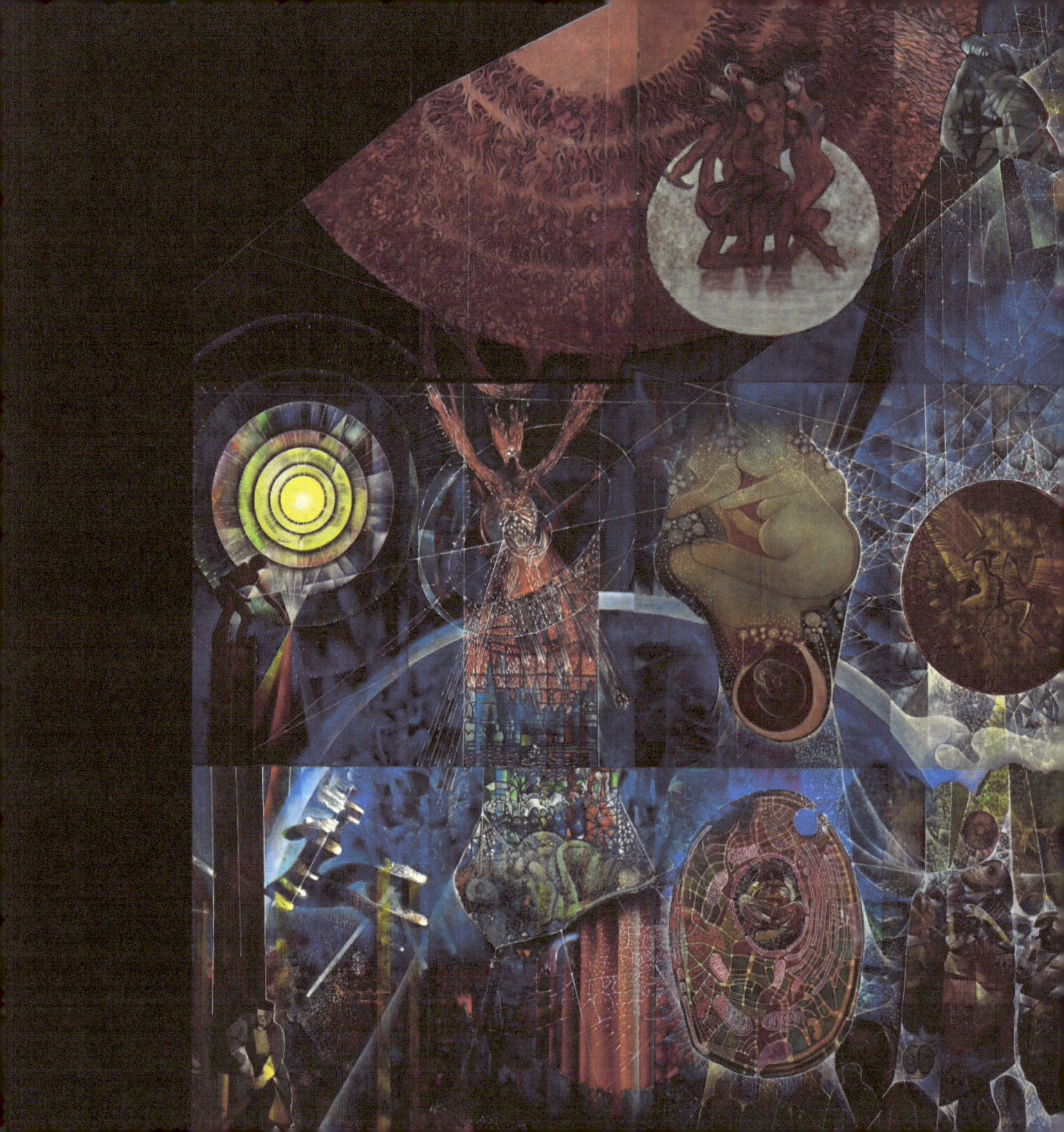

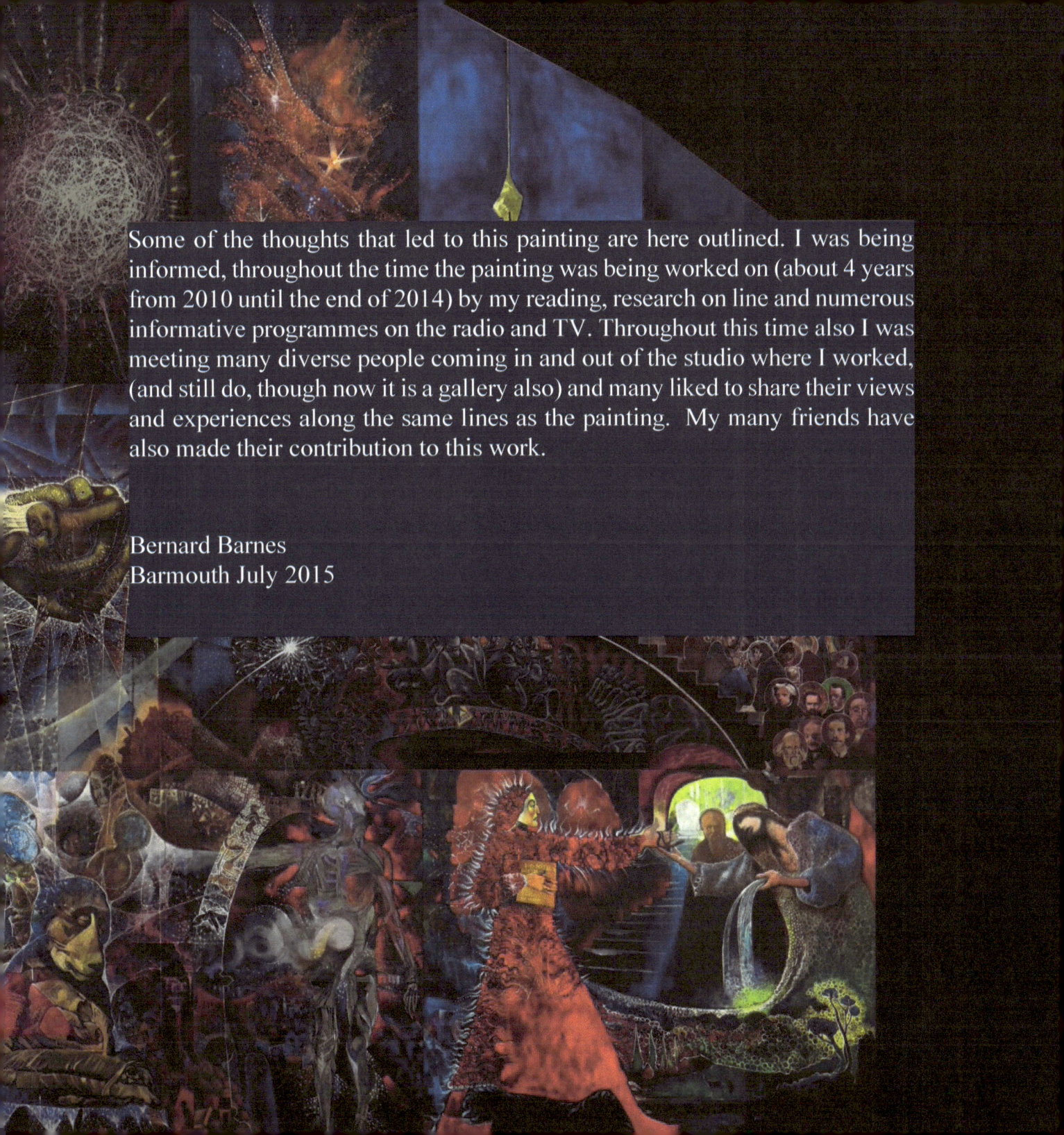

Some of the thoughts that led to this painting are here outlined. I was being informed, throughout the time the painting was being worked on (about 4 years from 2010 until the end of 2014) by my reading, research on line and numerous informative programmes on the radio and TV. Throughout this time also I was meeting many diverse people coming in and out of the studio where I worked, (and still do, though now it is a gallery also) and many liked to share their views and experiences along the same lines as the painting. My many friends have also made their contribution to this work.

Bernard Barnes
Barmouth July 2015

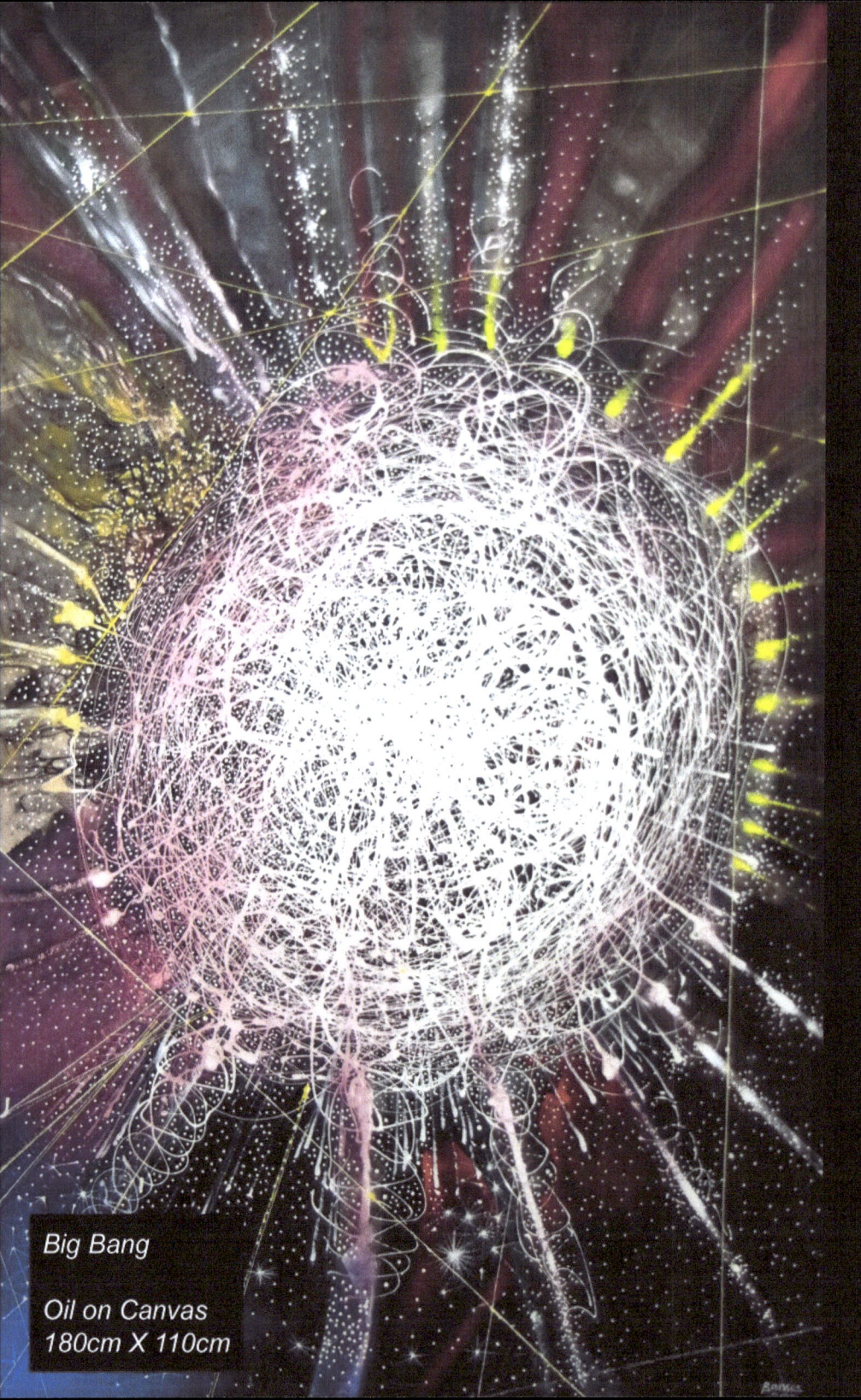

Big Bang

Oil on Canvas
180cm X 110cm

The Great Singularity

The discovery that the universe was expanding (the Hubble Red Shift) led inevitably to the conclusion that once it had been smaller. Its origins must have had a beginning, and that beginning must have been 'a singularity'. All that was simple logic.

Since then science has arrived at a date (not so accurately determined as was Bishop Ushers' to the hour of the day of the month etc......) but accurate enough to say 13.7 billion years since the Big Bang.

That has become the standard model of the universe now adopted by most physicists and astrophysicists. However odd, counter intuitive, it seems that all of this immense universe, galaxy upon galaxy, was once packed into a single point.

It is like trying to portray God the Father, trying to paint the big bang. Physicists tell us that there would have been no light, so nothing to see, and anyway there was no where else to be but inside it, because all of space and time was packed up there and nowhere else.

Nevertheless, the narrative of the large painting needed a starting point, and this picture is it. It denotes that the rest of the work will proceed from that canvas, and begin to explore the most bizarre story that could be told, the story of our universe.

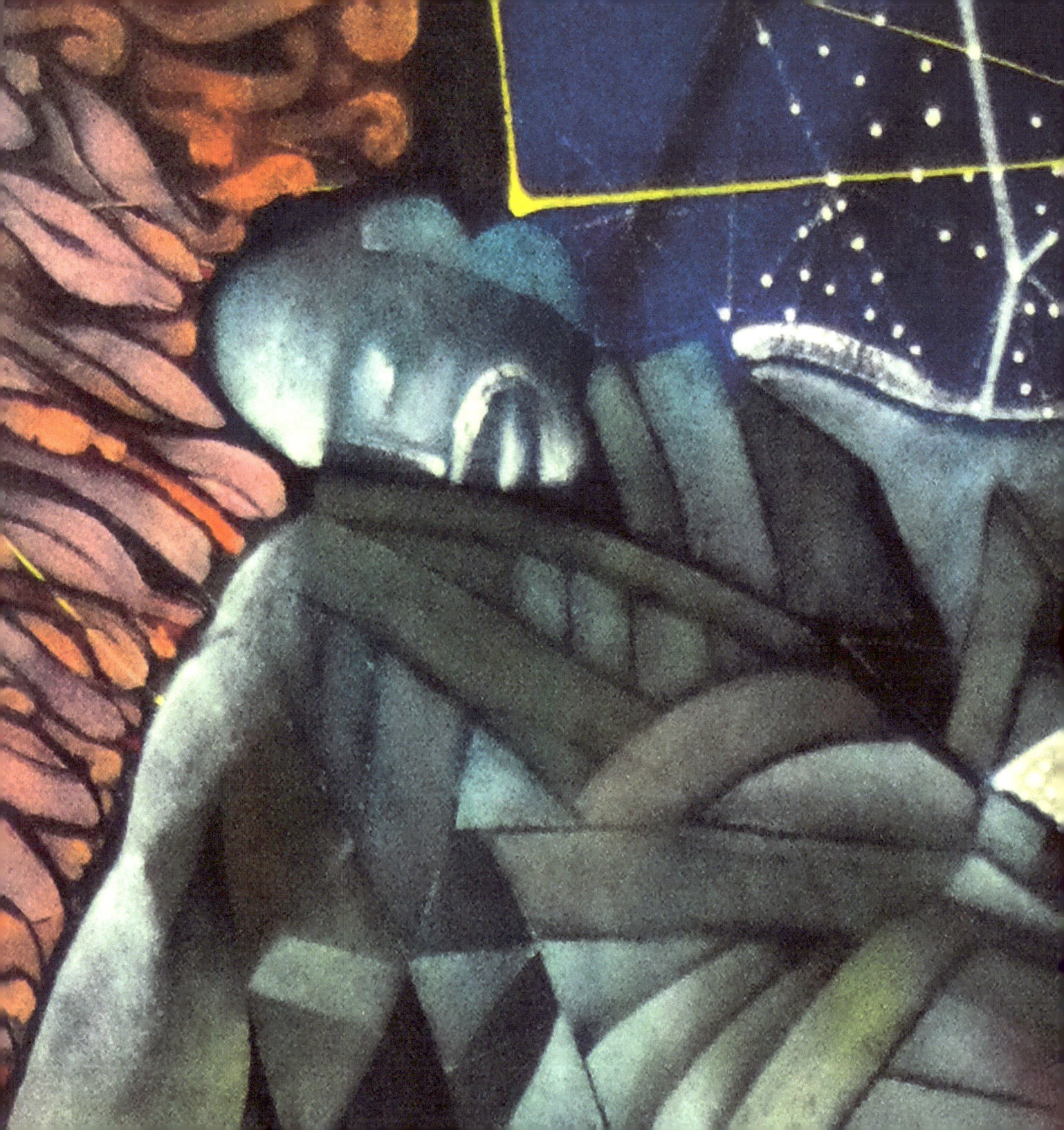

Hydrogen

It is said by cosmologists that the state of the universe immediately after the big bang was that of a plasma of electrons, protons and photons out of which, after 378,000 years it cooled to a point that favoured the formation of hydrogen, the first and simplest of the atoms.

Shortly after this another event called 'decoupling' occurred when the photons broke away from matter and began to travel freely throughout the universe. These photons do not interact with matter and they form the Cosmic Background Radiation of the universe.

At this point, light appears, worthy of a painting by mad John Martin.

The electromagnetic forces that act upon the constituent particles of matter became possible only when the temperatures had cooled. A proton binds with an electron in a vicelike embrace, throughout the fabric of the universe, hydrogen began to form out of the plasma.

This painting was made with these thoughts in mind. I took the image of a bound figure, with a suggestion of wings to express the new state of being in the universe, the first binding of matter.

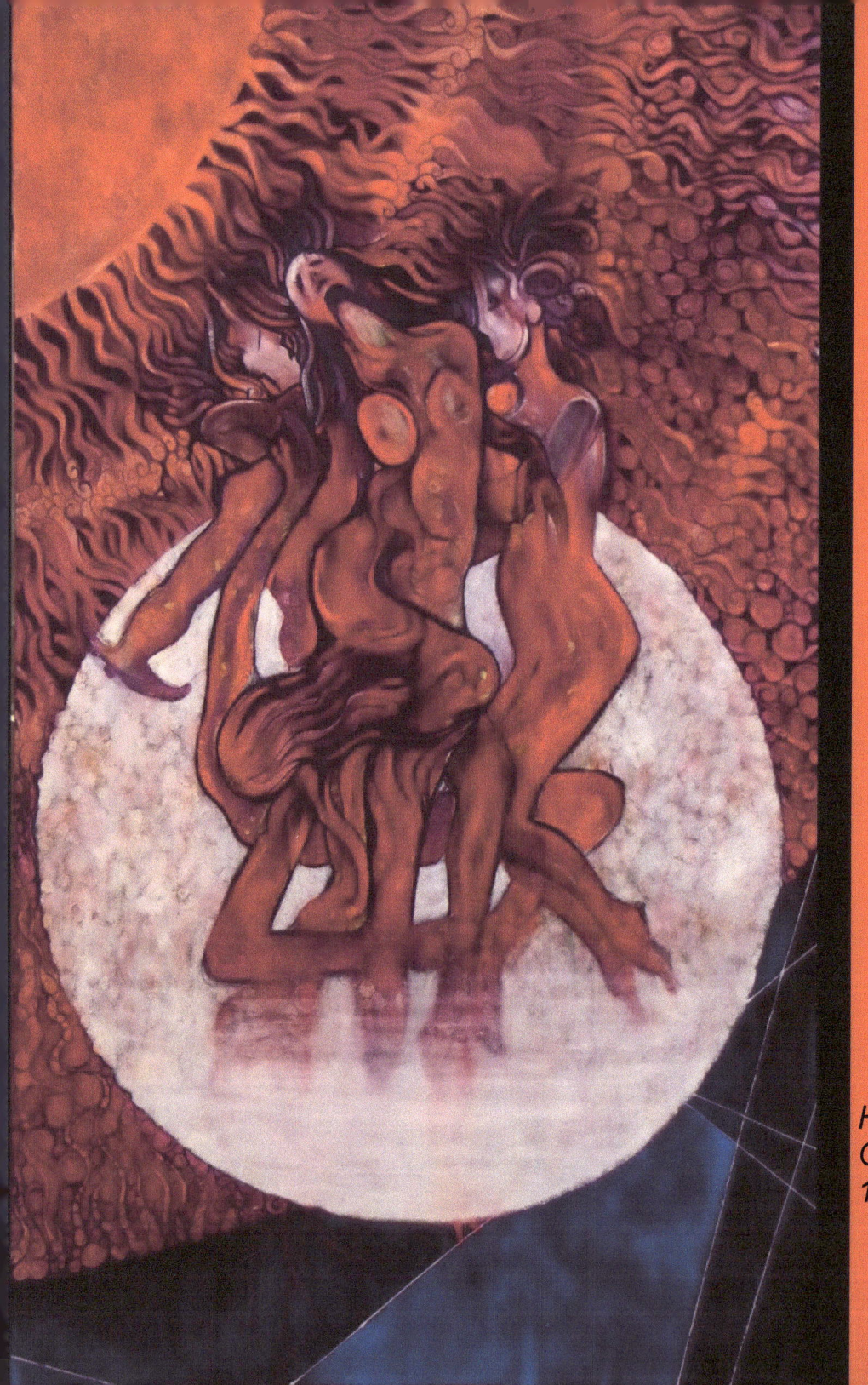

Helium
Oil on canvas
180cm x 110cm

Helium

We are told that over the next 300,000 years the expansion continued and cooled to a temperature of 10,000°K.

Two protons and neutrons each bonded in the inferno to produce the atomic nuclei of helium. Another atom had now been forged, this time made of hydrogen atoms.

The new atom, with a heavier centre and two orbiting electrons curiously is lighter than the sum of two hydorgen atoms. In the process of binding, heat and light is shed as the first hydrogen stars bust into nuclear fusion. Such a star is our own sun.

These stars are burning their hydrogen over a lifecycle of billions of years. The paintings will explore these developments, in so far as we know them.

I chose to anthropomorphise helium as a group of writhing figures against the backdrop of a bright white burning hydrogen star. That star is our own sun.

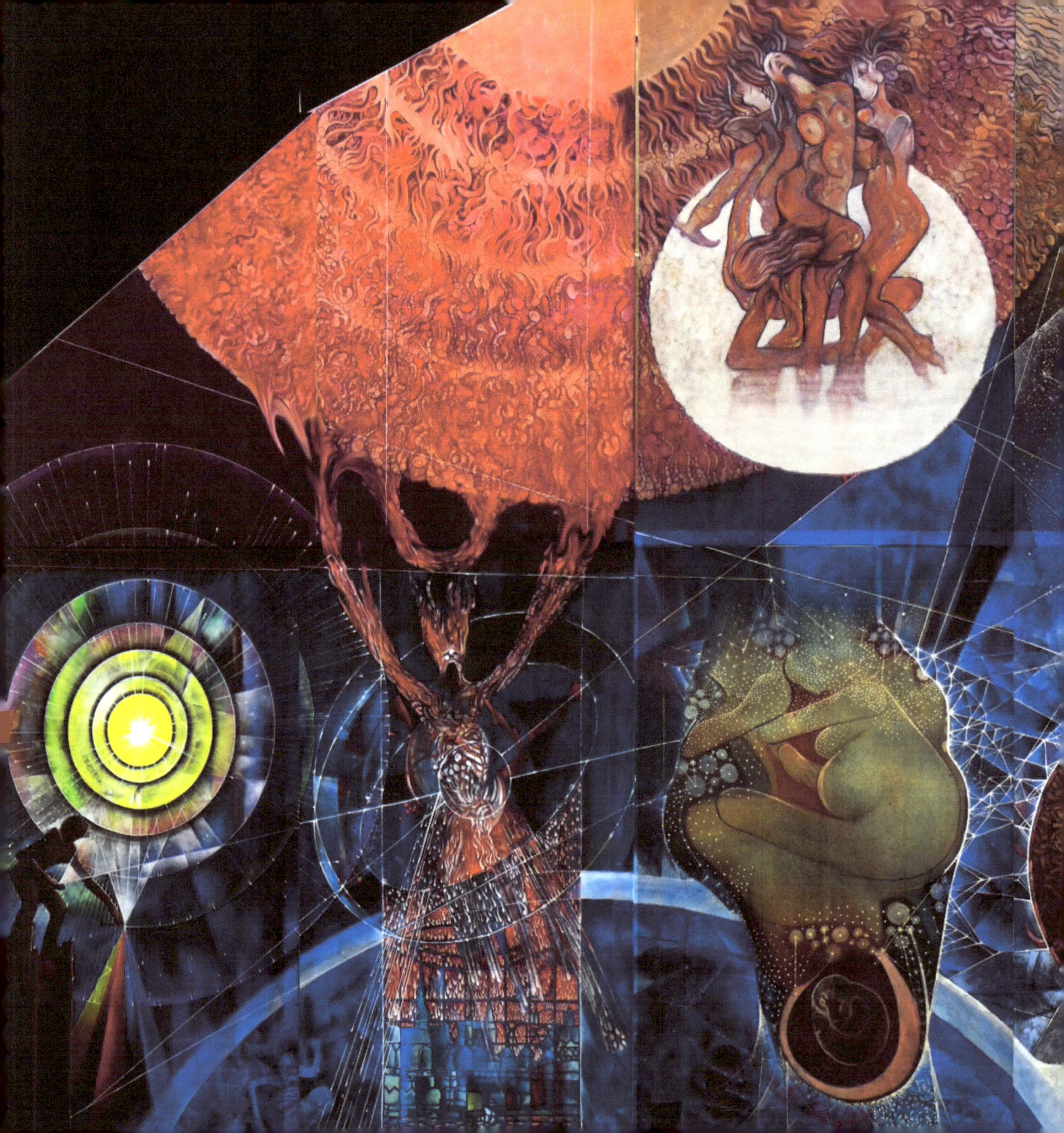

Red Giant Stars

The huge star in the background of the painting at this point is a red giant. Many times greater than our sun, this type of massive object burns the material of its composition (not just of hydrogen and helium, but debris from supernova explosions etc.) so fiercely that new atoms begin to be forged, right up to the molecular weight of iron (55) and nickel (58).

There are many types of these stars, with complex inner shells. All of this I have tried to express in the painting. They represent the great wombs of the universe, these stars, places where half of the atoms known in the universe are created.

You may be able to see vertical lines of slightly different colours descending the painting in this area, and below. These lines were painted with the different elements in mind, each of which has characteristic colours. It is interesting that the various colours used by a painter are the result of these elements and compounds of elements being brushed onto a surface.

Red Giant
Oil on canvas
180cm x 110cm

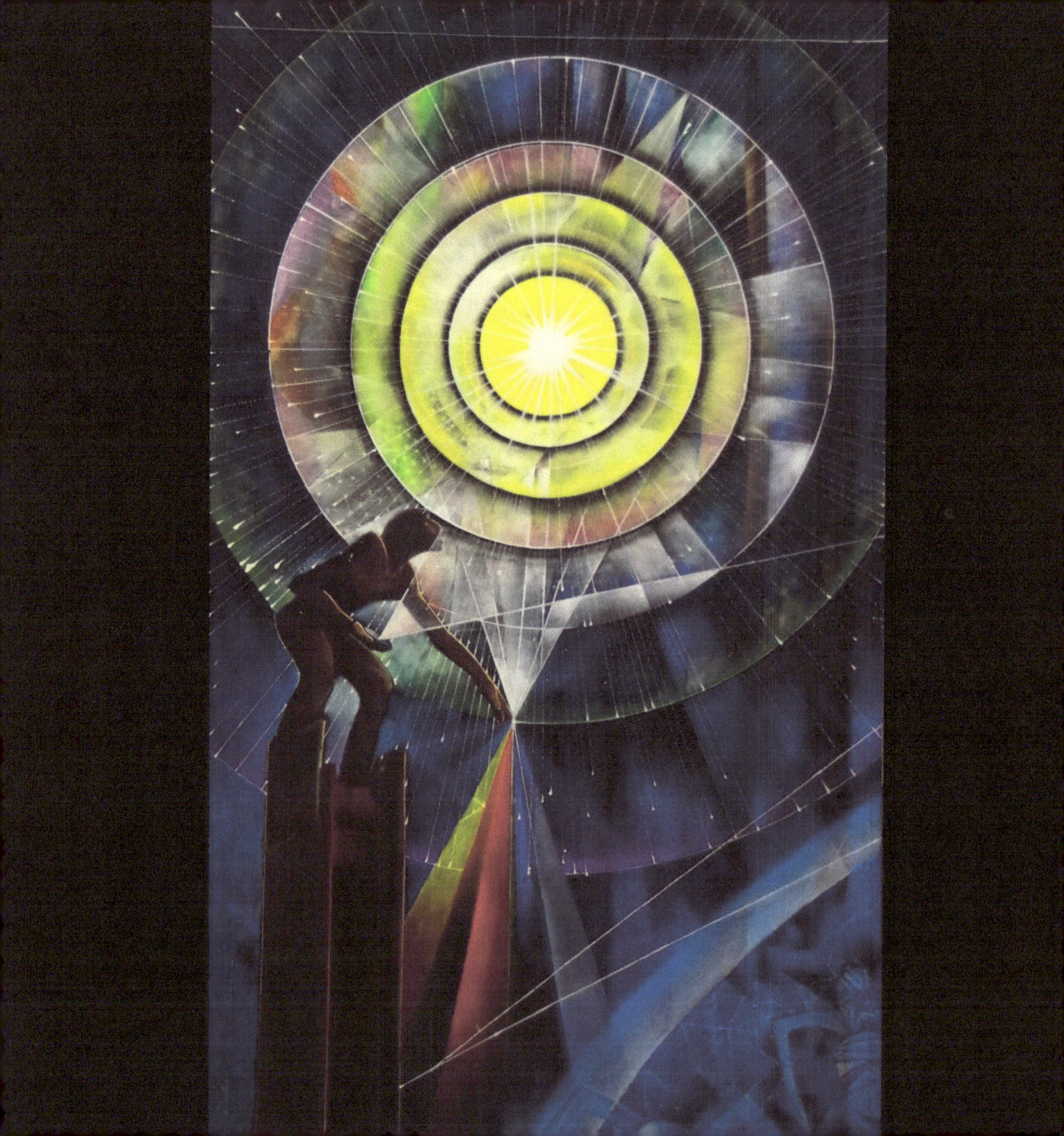

The Super Nova

The Red Giants reach the end of their lives in a variety of ways, according to the discoveries of astrophysicists. Examples of many of them are familiar to us through the Hubble Telescope. Some of these giants end up as a brilliantly hot tiny white star surrounded by an expanding shell of fragmented materials rich in all the elements of the old giant.

But one type of red giant of a particular size and composition explodes in a spectacular display of cosmic energy. These are the super-nova, the candles of the universe, always going off with the same intensity and degree of light production. Using these rare events (actually not so rare when you have the entire universe to search) astronomers are able to calculate distances in deep space.

In this inferno new atoms are added to the mélange, increasing the number to 118. If you read the literature, the scientists are able to describe the sequence of atomic linkages and rings that each element follows in the course of its formation.

This mass ejection of rich matter, mere dust from the great star, for great clouds of galactic material.

The primate like figure, balancing on the top of the iron column is witnessing a super nova. His finger (actually it requires a prism) is touching the light and splitting it into its component parts. Note also that he is holding a mirror that reflects the light from the supernova across the picture to an observatory on the highest peak.

This reference to the splitting of light is connected to the science of spectroscopy which has found that white light is a composite of light of different wavelengths. Using prisms and diffraction sheets it is now possible to 'read' the light. We can see bands of colour and lines, and tell the composition of the star (or any luminous source). This way we can read the stars.

Supernova
Oil on canvas
180cm x 110cm

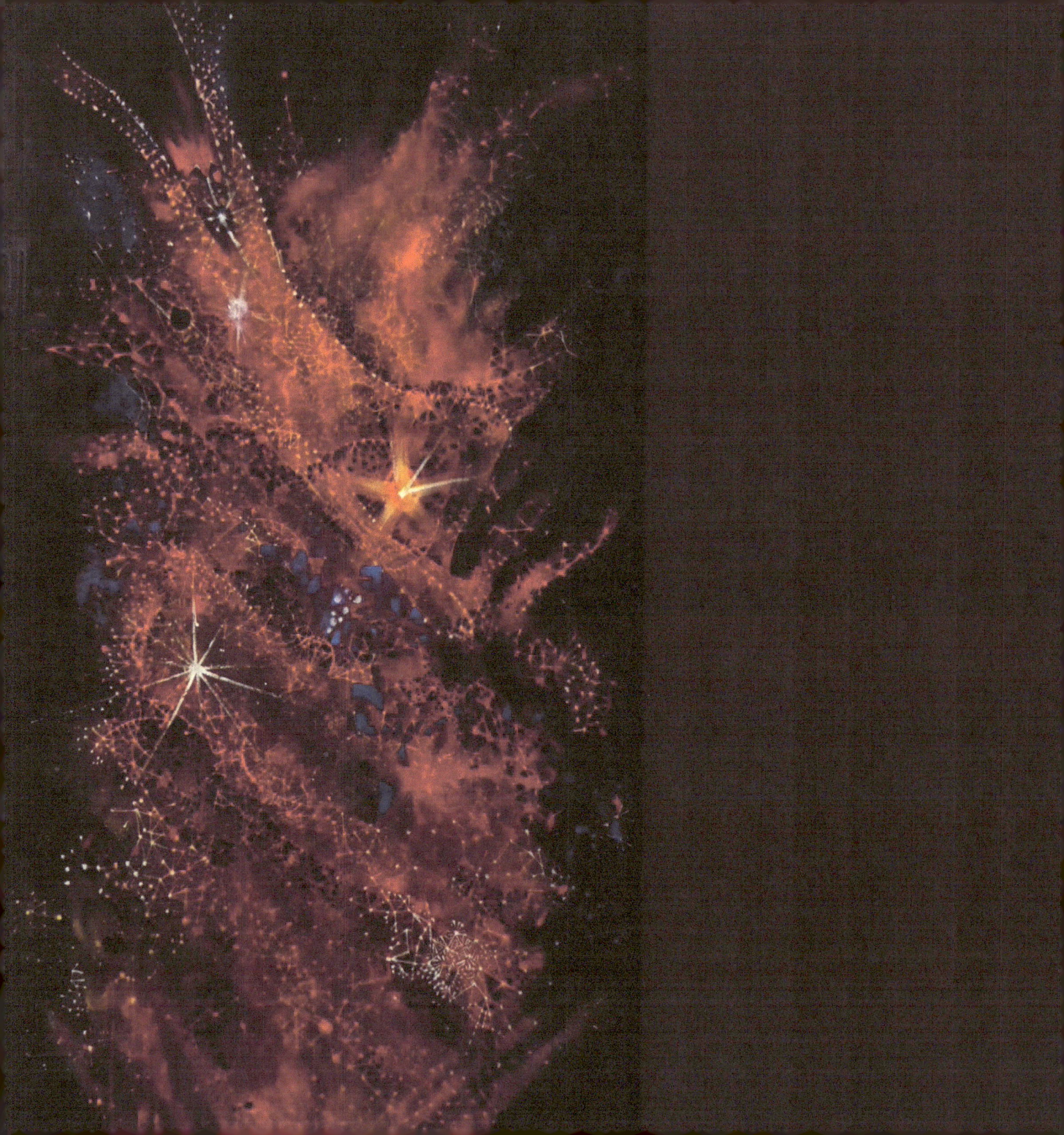

Nebula

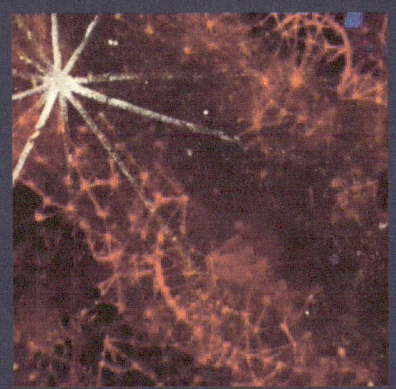

Until the true nature of galaxies were understood, thanks to Hubble and others, they were mislabelled as 'nebula'. So we have 'the Andromeda Nebula' commonly used to describe what is actually the Andromeda galaxy.

A Nebula is a vast gas cloud, sometimes hundreds of light years across, made of hydrogen, helium and other ionised gases. These clouds have very low mass, less dense than any earthly created vacuum, but here and there within them the effects of gravity gradually brings them together into clouds of greater density.

As these clouds of gas and dust clump together they gain in mass and therefore gravity raising the temperature in the centre. When this temperature rise reaches sufficient intensity the cloud will burst into fusion and a new star is born.

Sometimes it requires a nudge in the fabric of space, a gravitational nudge, to start the process of star formation. A supernova explosion, it is thought, may have the igniting effect. This means that as a great star dies in its final convulsion it may spark a new star into existence elsewhere in space.

Nebula
Oil on canvas
180cm x 110cm

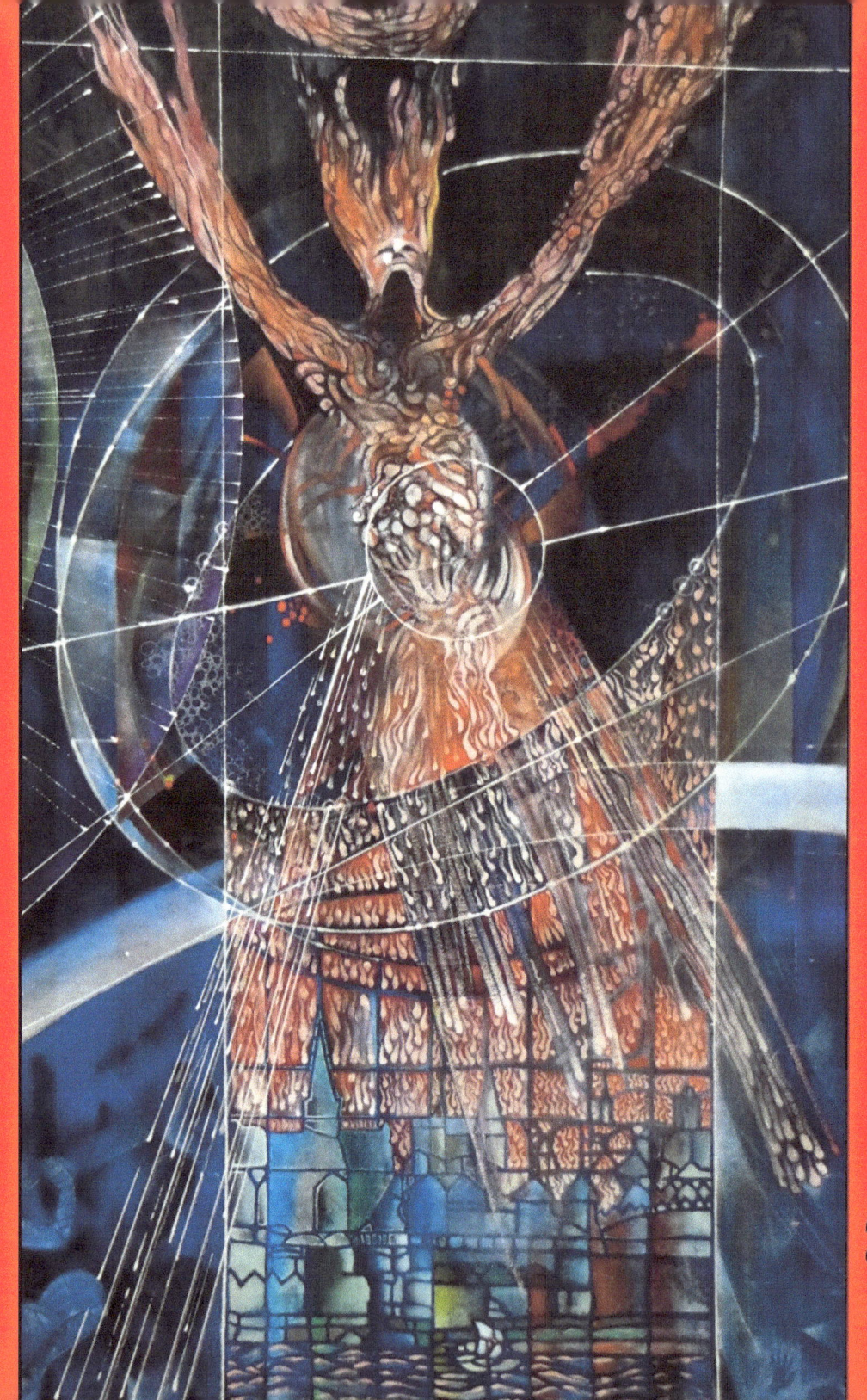

Iron
Oil on canvas
180cm x 110cm

Iron

The centre of the earth is just 3,958.8 miles under our feet. Down there, about 70% the size of the moon is an inner core of iron and nickel. A core 2,100 miles in radius of molten iron and other materials is below us too.

Most of the material that forms the slag of the planet as it has cooled and crystallised, subject to pressure and cleavage, erosion and innundation is also composed of iron. It is not surprising that our own culture is practically built on the same material.

Iron has a molecular weight of 56 and nickel of 58 that formed the limit of the element forming cycle in the dense red giant stars. The accumulation of molten compressed iron at the core of these stars, left over from the chain of interactions and fusions that had burned the star's helium away, became the stuff that eventually snuffed the stars out. It was certainly flung far and wide into interstellar space by the resulting supernova.

Great belts of fragments can be seen around planets, like the rings of Saturn, and around solar systems, like the Kuiper belt around our own. Much of this material are lumps of metal from the heart of those giant stars. When a piece of this material enters our own atmosphere it usually burns up. When the earth was forming it was subject to a continuous barrage of similar events as the small planet hoovered up the debris in its district. In those days the sky must have rained with falling stars. Such a phenomena has been witnessed in Trinidad, when the sky was so full of falling asteroids that it looked like rain.

So here, in this painting, I imagine Iron as a burning figure existential as a roaring flame thrown out of the red giant and showering burning iron down onto the earth. I have dramatized the event to make it appear as a bombardment of iron onto a medieval city. Many medieval cities did experience similar bombardments, though that iron was cast by their enemies.

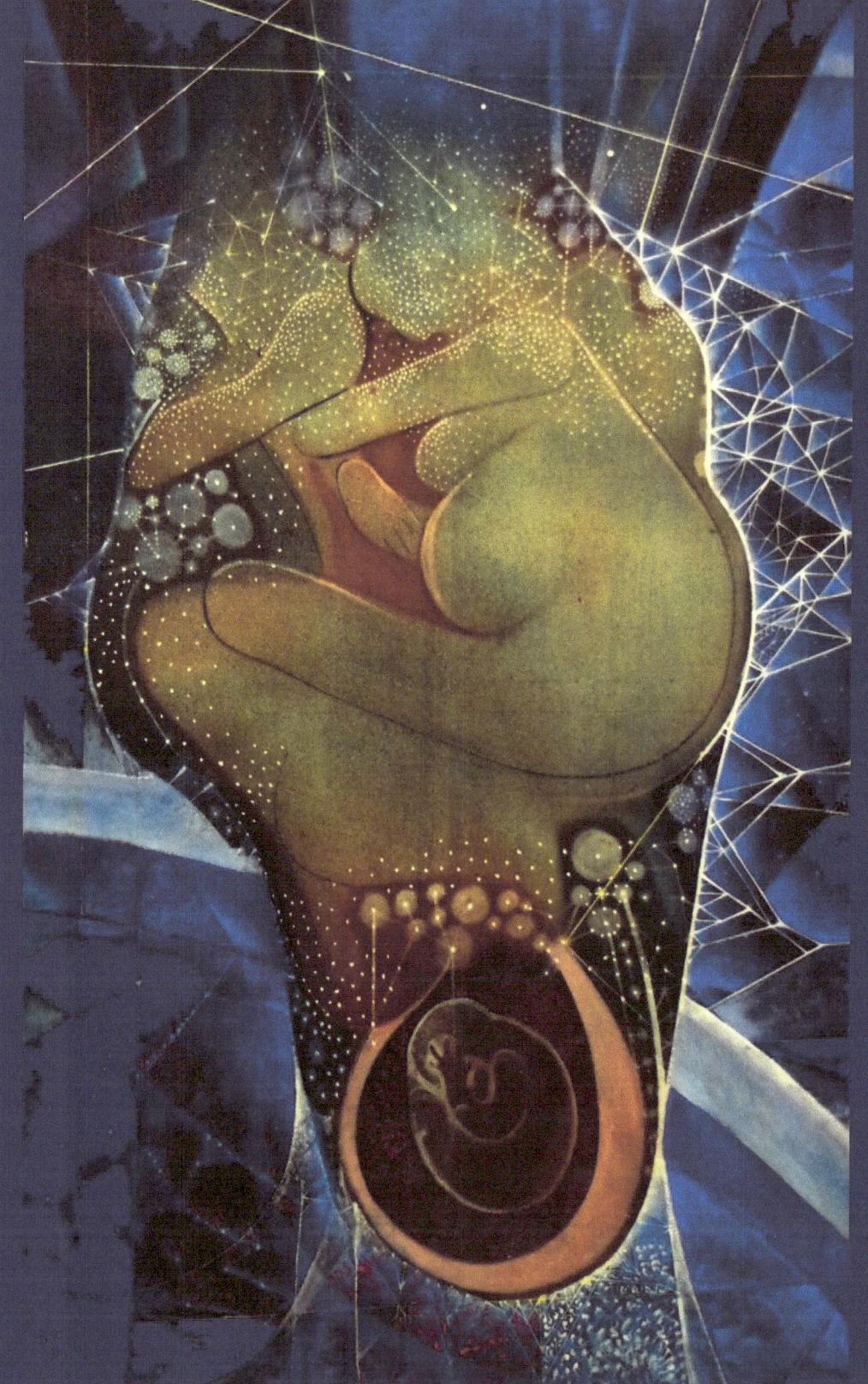

Replication
Oil on canvas
180cm x 110cm

Replication

A single being made of two separate beings (a fundamental paradox). This phenomena of doubling recalls the process of embryonic growth from single cell to blastula etc. Notice the pendant creatures in their thousand hanging below this figure like bats in a cave.

The figure is pregnant. Hanging below in amniotic bliss, the fetus is slowly coming to life.

The overall feeling of this picture is blissful, ecstatic and peaceful. The fetus will soon give birth to many. Fecundity.

This is the great force of life like a strong wind blowing. Desire consumes us, a fire in a wind. We do not will our desires, our desires will us. It is one of the greatest of the many forces that are continuously acting upon the individual.

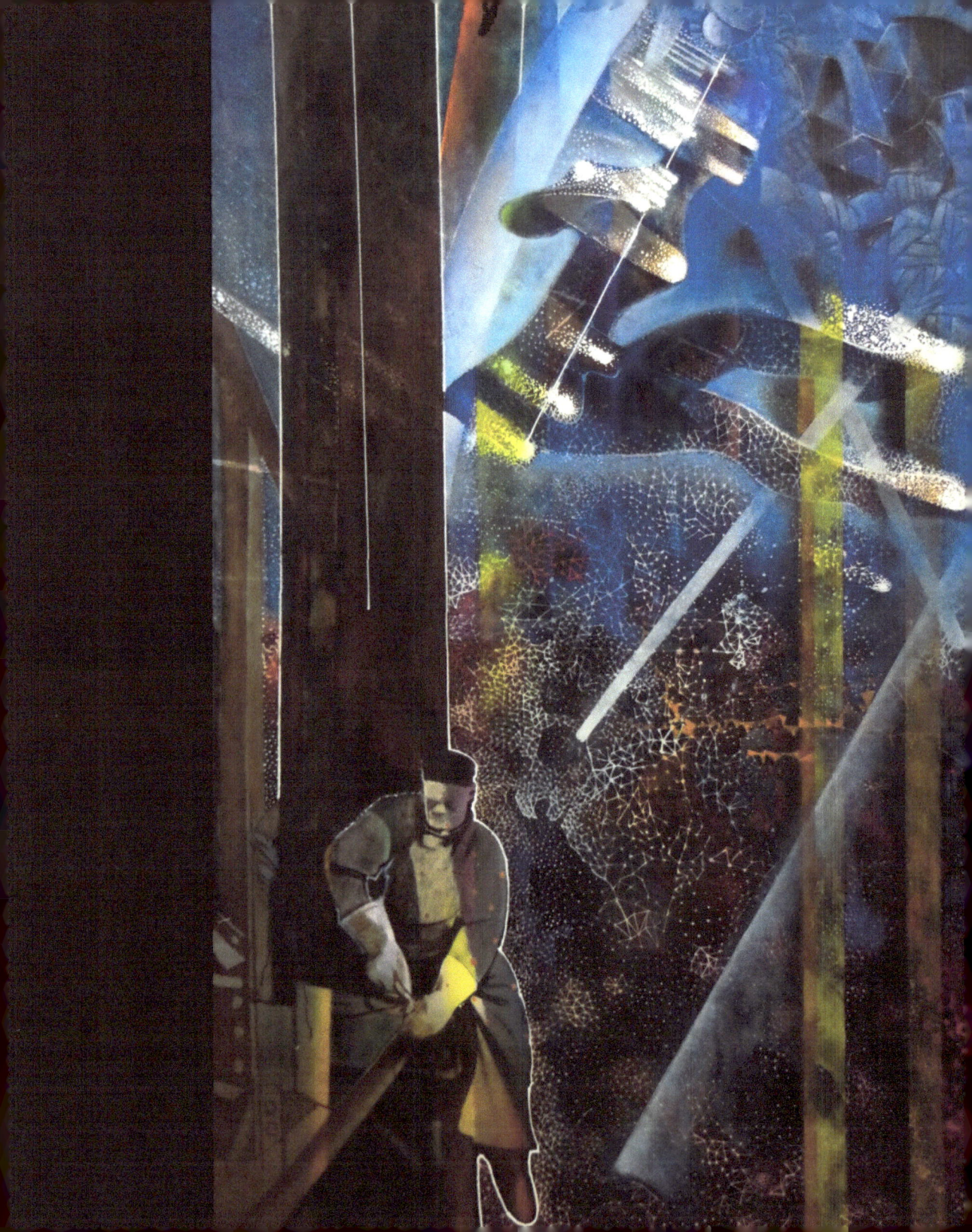

Pigment and Chemistry

Every colour in the painter's palette is a chemical. Looking along the shelves of a colourman's shop is looking at the variety of rock that are found in the earth's crust; Gypsum, stibnite, gelina, graphite, cinnabar, hematite, malachite, azurite and so on. These are all part of the earth's crust.

These are all part of the earth.

The Iron City

Here the picture shows the iron city made by steel erectors. Iron forms the 'last burn' of the red giant stars as they used up the remaining hydrogen in the core. All the heavier elements after iron were formed, it is thought, in the increadable heat of a super-nova.

The verticle lines that are faintly visible in this part of the picture are all tinted different colours to indicate the different elements, there are 118 here on earth. Everything is made from them.

Notice also the signs of war, the searchlights, throwing out lines of light, of photons, into space. Some of those photons may continue travelling outwards endlessly.

Steel Erector
oil on canvas
180cm x 110cm

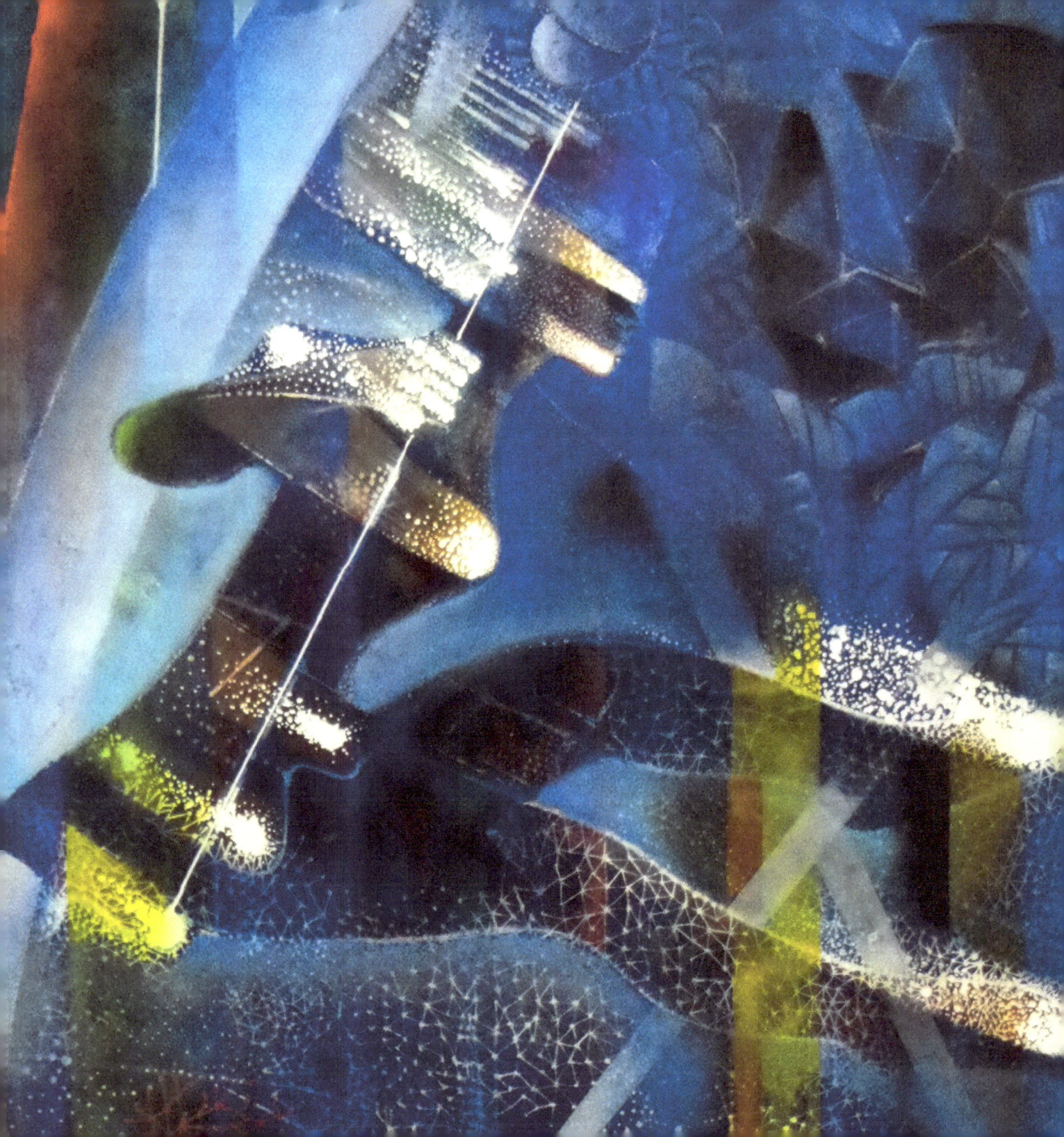

Comets

I imagine an acrobat, dressed like an angel, swinging in on her trapeze. She is made from comets.

It is thought that many of these celestial objects are composed primarily of water ice, and may have rained down onto earth so heavily as to form the oceans.

That's some rainstorm.

Detail from Iron City

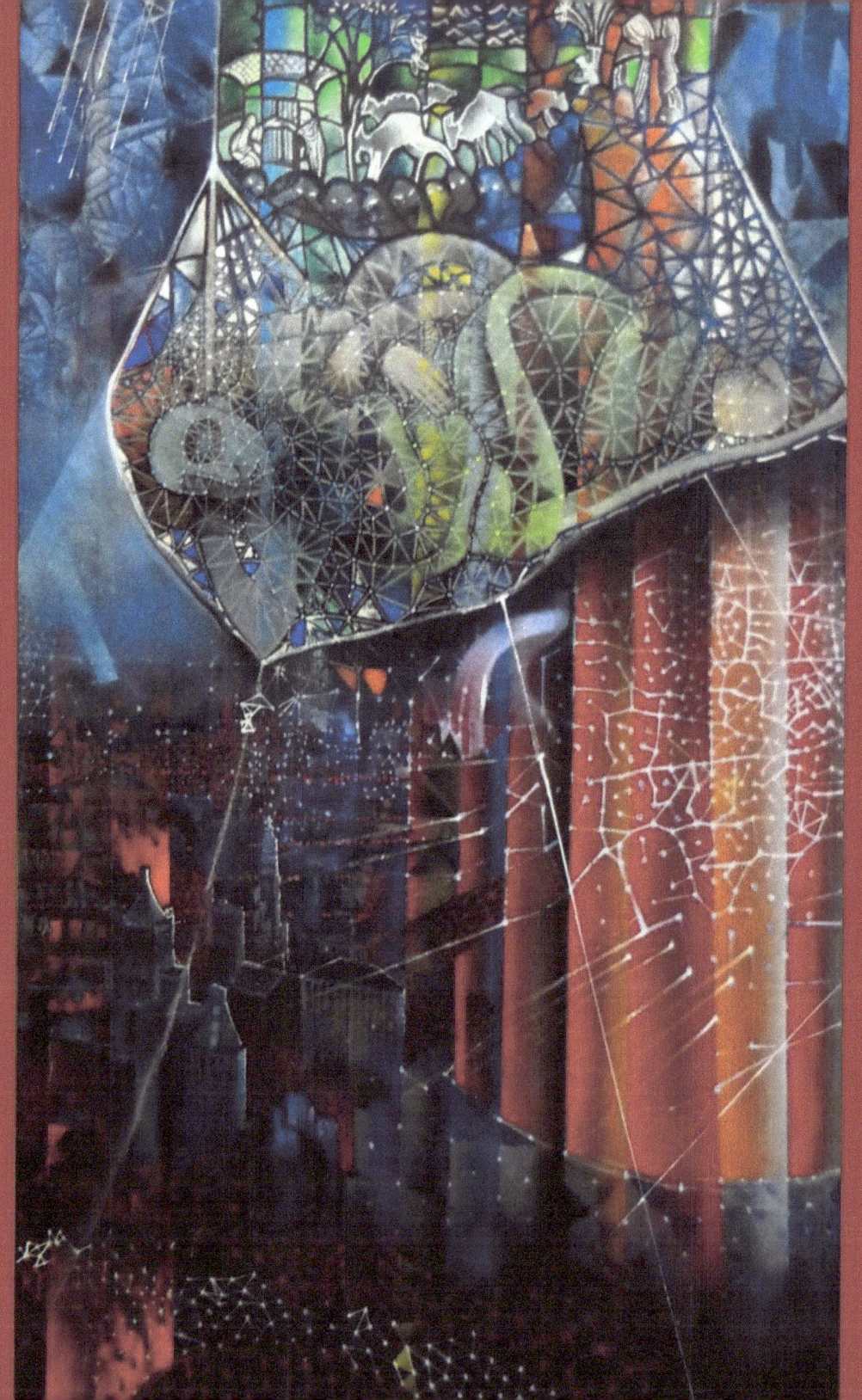

Dreamers

There is a net hanging down. It is filled with dreaming figures, above them are their beatific dreams, dreaming their cities.

In reality the medieval city (painted in a style influenced by stained glass) is being bombarded by a cascade of meteors. It is interesting to reflect that some cities often were bombarded by iron (the same iron that fell out of the sky as meteors).

These meteors are depicted as proceeding from a huge fiery figure, my representation of iron. Among the balls that are falling are trails of nickel, sodium, phosphate etc.

Dreamers
Oil on canvas
180cm x 110cm

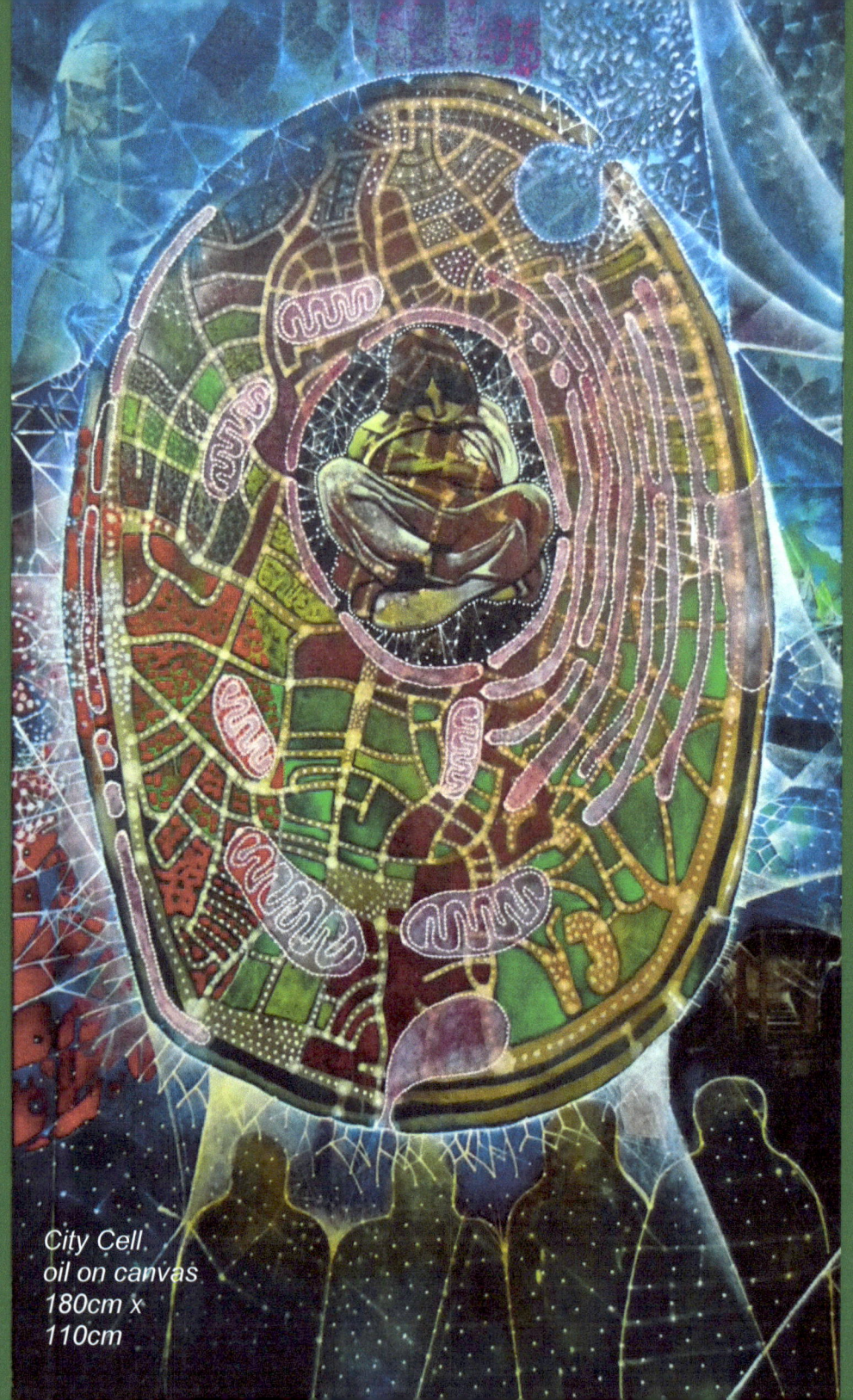

City Cell
oil on canvas
180cm x
110cm

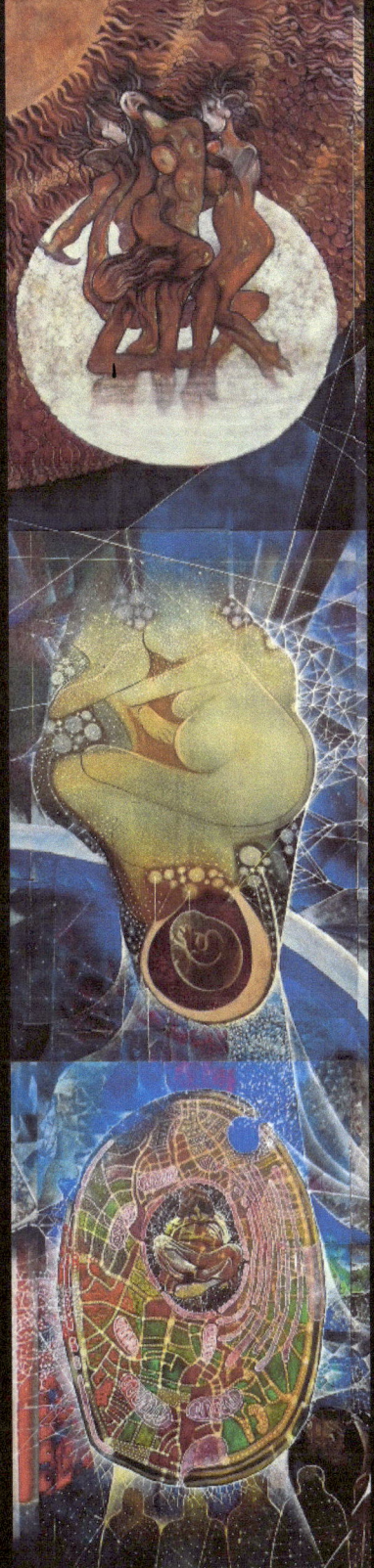

City Cell

Is a sort of egg, appropriate if you remember that it comes below the painting of replication. It is, in fact, a map of medieval Bruge. Have a look at it on Google if you don't know its organic form. I have squashed it somewhat in order to fit it into the rather idiosyncratic shape of the canvases.

Over this city I have superimposed the diagram of a eukariote cell. You may see the membrane, the mitochondria, the endoplasmic reticulum, the nucleus. Inside the nucleus, as though imprisoned, is a human (who was in fact a South American mummy).

There is a connection between the two. I have developed this idea in my book 'City as Superorganism' where other paintings are used to illustrate some of these ideas.

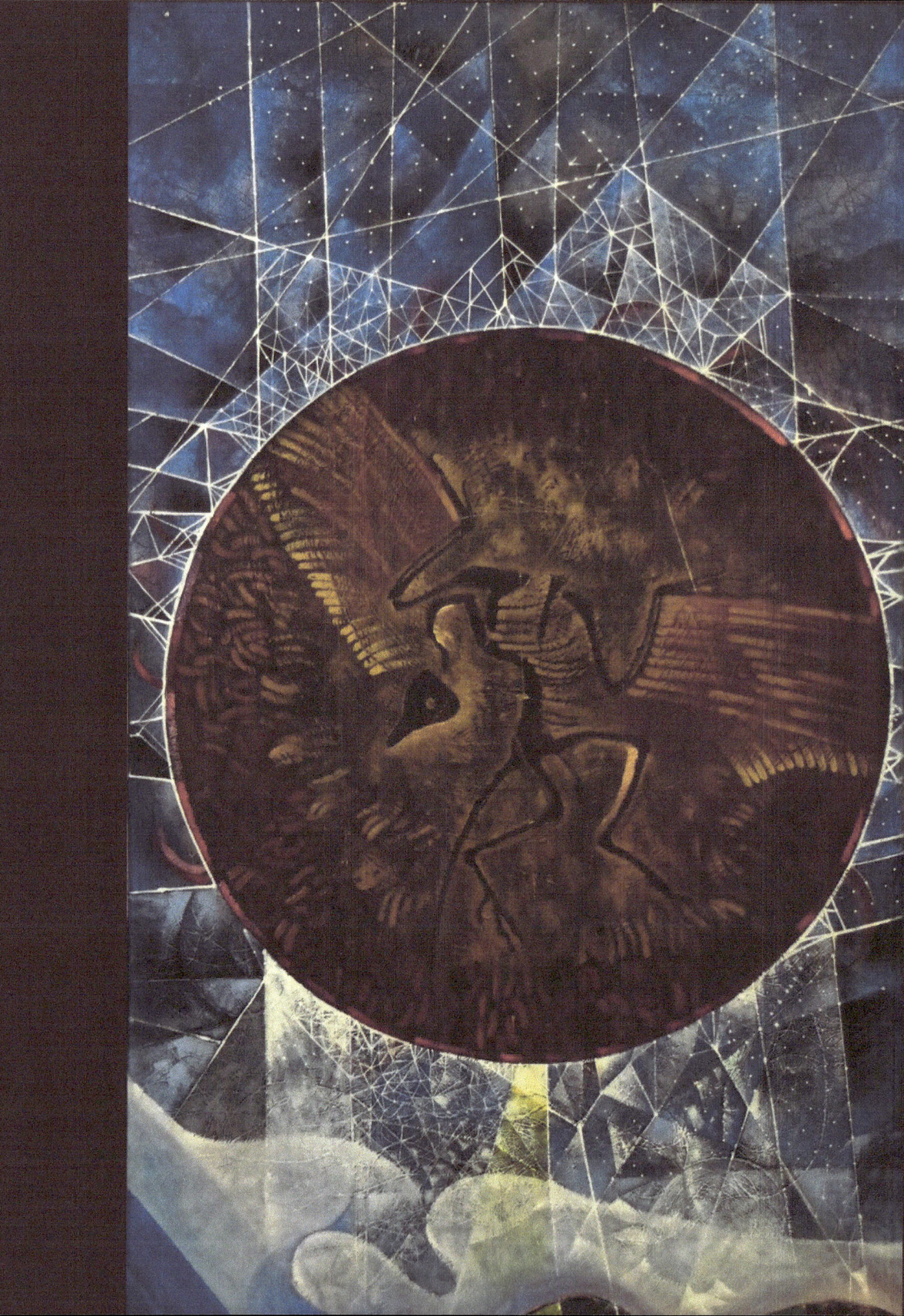

Central Panel

This panel is still being reserved for development, in the centre of the picture, that presently depicts Australopithecus (the proto-bird). It is lying shattered on a sort of lunar landscape. I have Icarus in my mind here I suppose.

I have long thought that this area could be used for occasional projections – within the circle of the moon. I have conceived of a projection of the burning sun here, one I once saw in Bilbao, projected onto a ceiling. Ideally the sun should be the actual sun, but in Wales it is so intermittently visible that I fear it would not be practicable.

Archaeopteryx
Oil on canvas
180cm x 110cm

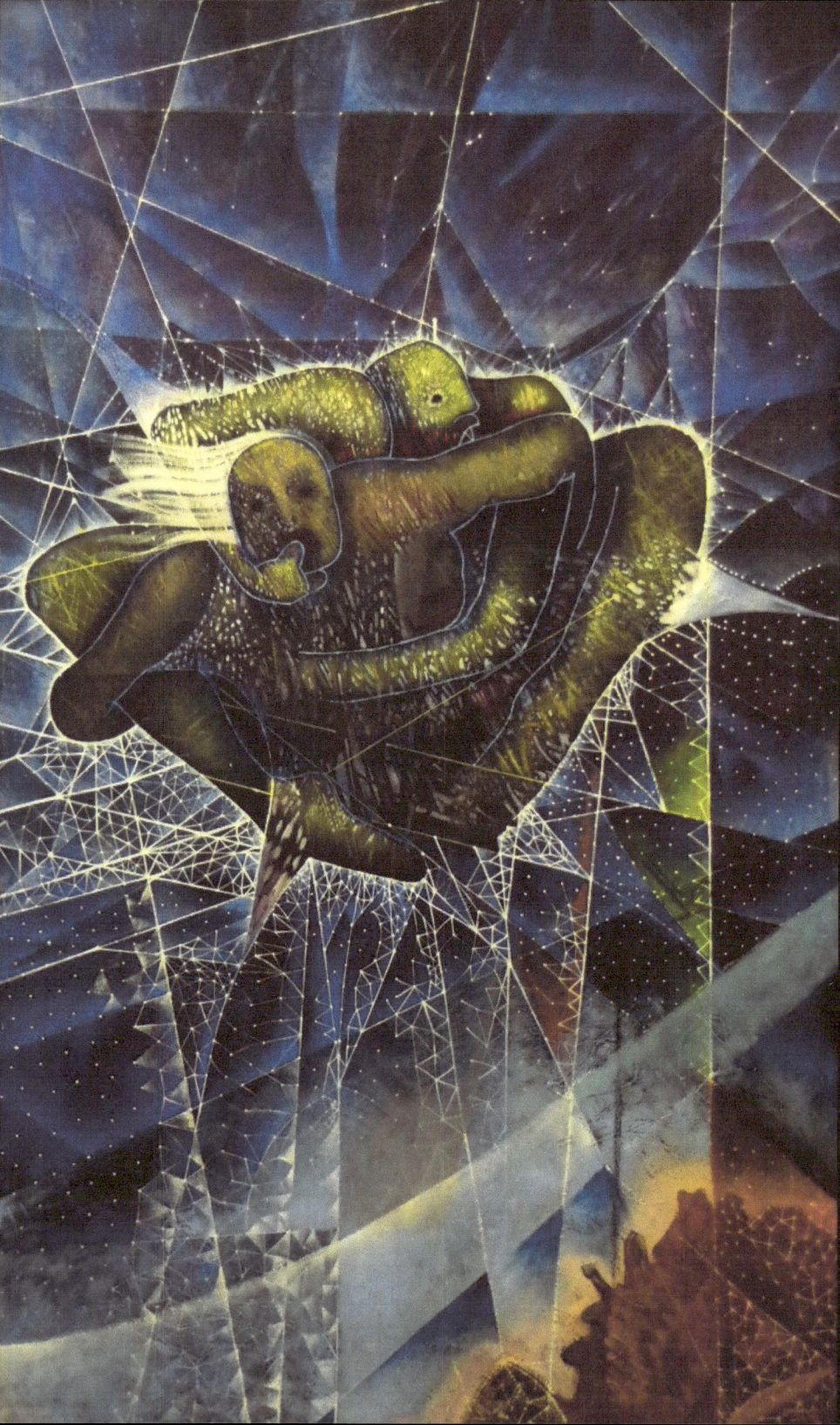

Quantum Flux

Here matter is continuously being destroyed by antimatter. We witness the disintegration in an almost Blakian representation.

This extraordinary drama is continuously happening, even in empty space so the physicists tell us. Out of nowhere come these particles, negative and positive, instantly annihilating each other in a faint burst of gamma radiation. These faint burst resound throughout the universe giving it a latent energy.

Quantum Flux
oil on canvas
180cm x 110cm

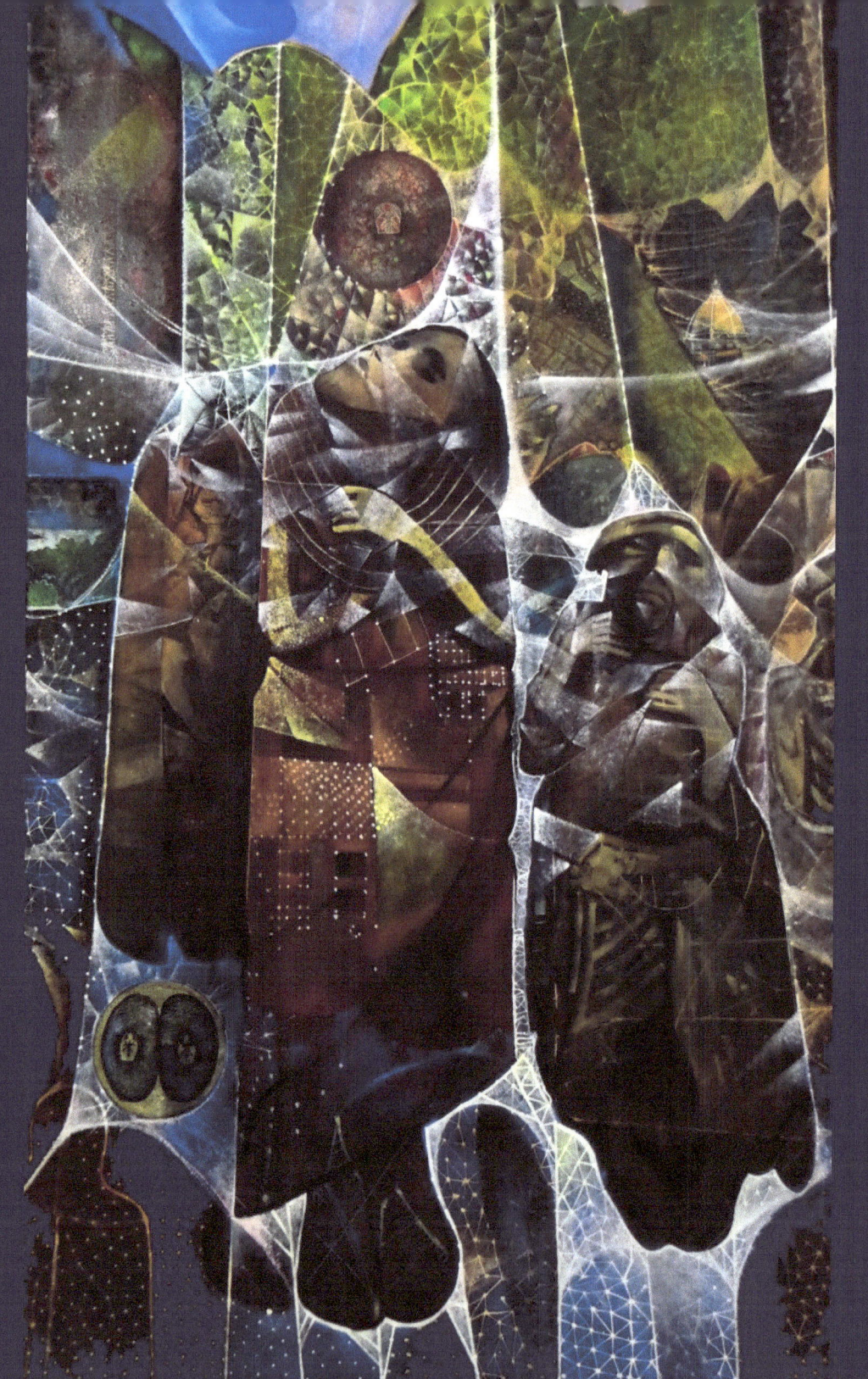

The Ancestors

I have been intrigued by these ancient mummified figures. Three of them (below Archaeopteryx) were found in the Gobi desert in an extraordinary 2,000 year old settlement.

These people had Caucasian features though they are far in the east, (so far indeed that the modern Chinese are reluctant to admit that the earliest settlers of that region were not Han Chinese).

One of their number was a woman of outstanding beauty and distinction, the beauty of Loulan. Others of her number hang beside her. Here and there is a space that looks as though it has been constructed by a spider. The connecting lines between objects are loose, like dust laden webs, not straight and electrical as in everywhere else in the picture.

Tucked within folds in this part of the painting are references to many cultural artefacts and references; The Duomo in Florence, Inside the Agia Sophia, Megista Lavra, Aggamemnon, landscapes and diagrams of various kinds.

I suppose the painting is abut the antiquity of human culture, its complexity too.

The beauty of
Loulan

Oil on canvas
180cm x 110cm

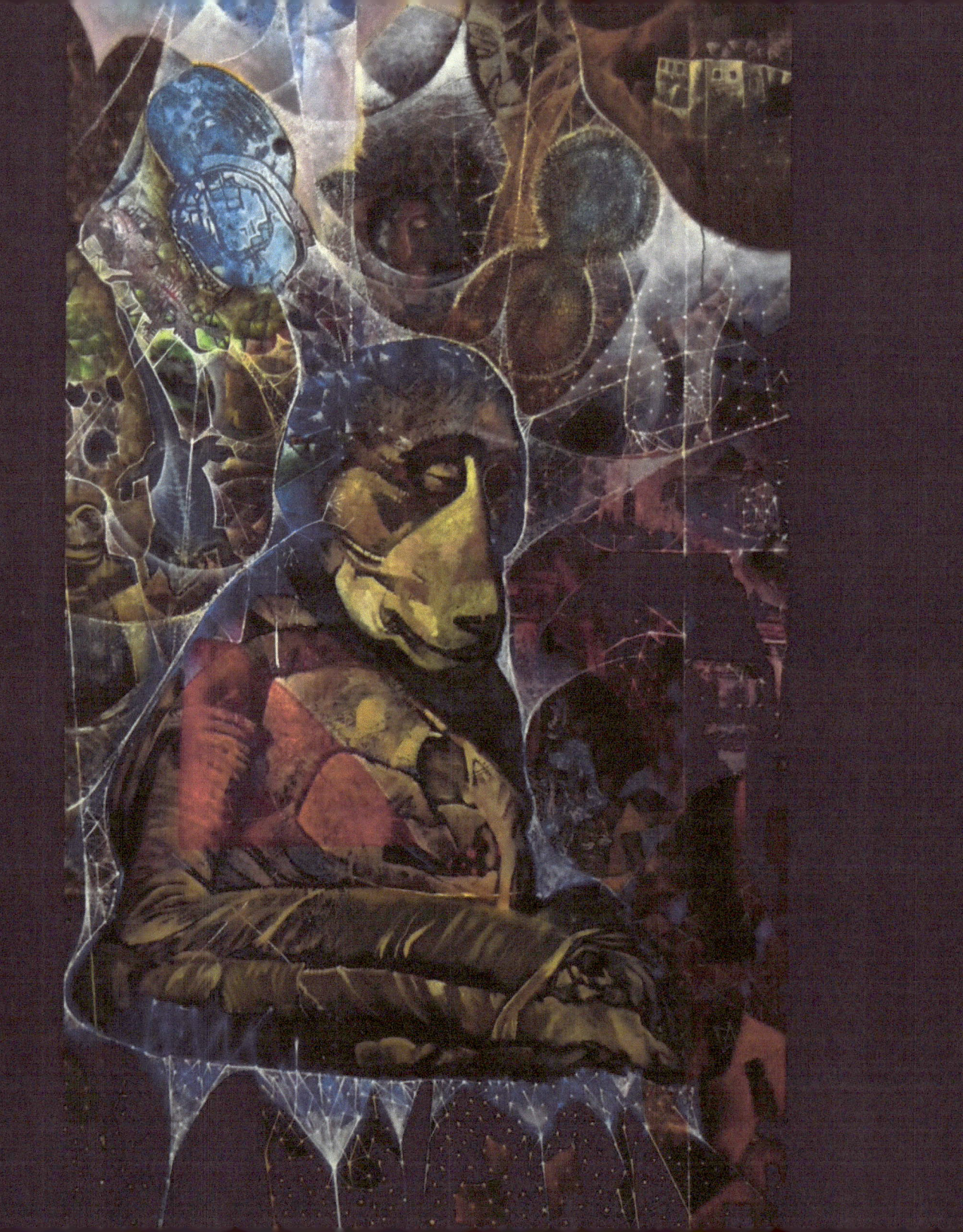

Primate

This baboon was maybe once the plaything of a pharoah. He now sits in a glass case in Egypt. He also sits here, swathed in cobwebs, dried out, light as the wind, dispersing in infinitely small fragments.

There is, beside him, a column of evolving animals. There is a classical painting of great temples by Claude Lorrain, along with various gothic architectural references.

Agamemnon can be seen above him, almost buried in caverns of web. A marriage ceremony, in diagramatic form, is taking place above his head,

It is an odd picture, in suspension. We are entering, with this canvas into a consideration of death.

Pharonic Baboon
oil on canvas
180cm x 110cm

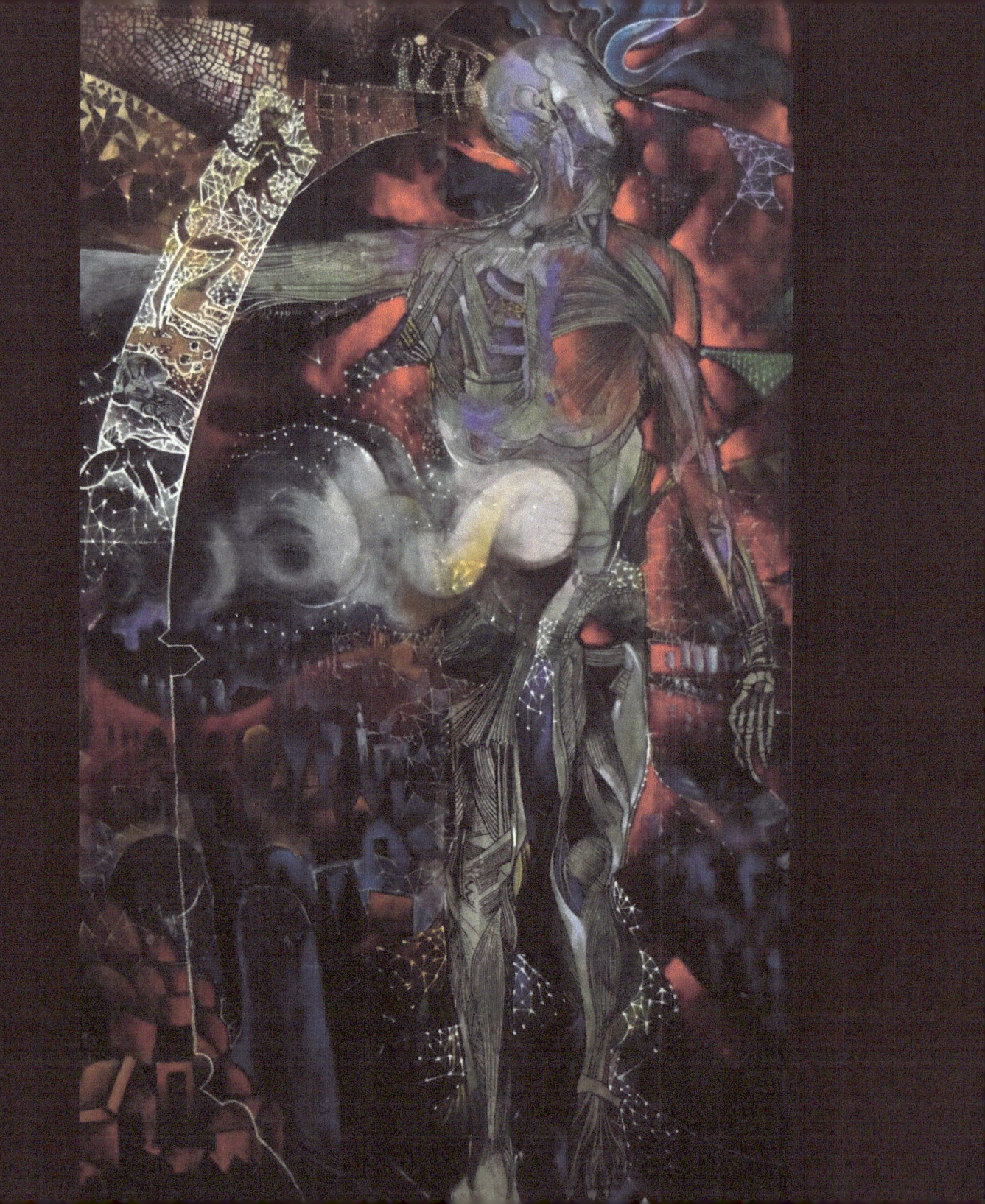

Decomposing Man

A man decomposes inside the arch, against a background of the uncountable dead. The figure is a composite of limbs reassembled from Grey's anatomy. This composite body represents 'everybody'. Here the painting explores the way the bodies disperse, gaseous, liquid and solid, broken down by fungi and consumed by insects. The complex parts returning to their origin, the earth.

Behind this figure is a world of shadows and memorials, now forgotten. Ranks of gravestones from the First World War, memories of that extraordinary Jewish cemetery in Prague (now cleaned of its piles of stones), the wasteland. Here is the medieval underworld, the Greek shades, the Jewish Gehenna, the Christian Hell and Purgatory. All of them pits of the human mind.

Decomposing man

oil on canvas
180cm x 110cm

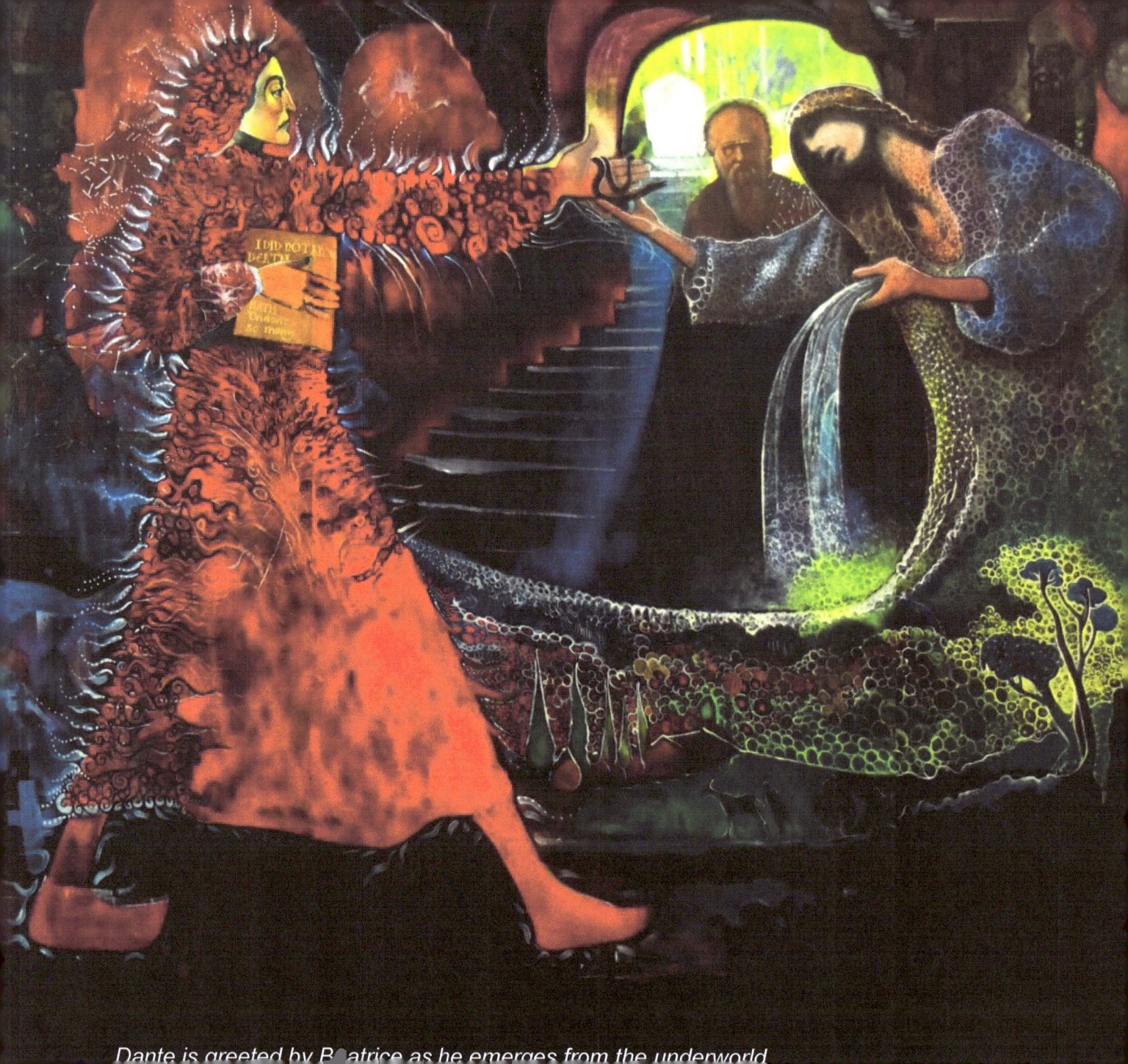

Dante is greeted by Beatrice as he emerges from the underworld

Dante

From this underworld of ignorance and superstition steps
a burning man, Dante emerging from his journey with
Virgil. He is carrying his 'Divine Comedy' bearing the
words (from T.S.Eliot 'I had not thought death had undone
so many…').

Dante is shown at the point of meeting Beatrice, his
beloved, when she will guide him through paradise. You
can see the latent sexual energy that licks from him, as
they touch for the first time. She is painted as a
superabundant being made of a host of beings – another
reference to the idea of the superorganism, but this time
it is a reference to the trillions of cells who make up the
human body and the many trillions more who have hitch
hiked a lift on our bodies. Colonies within colonies.

The figure of Dante also makes reference to the enormous
energy that is locked up in the structure of all these living
cells. The energy binding all the atoms of a human being
is colossal ($E = mc^2$). It is enough to power the whole of
the USA for a year.

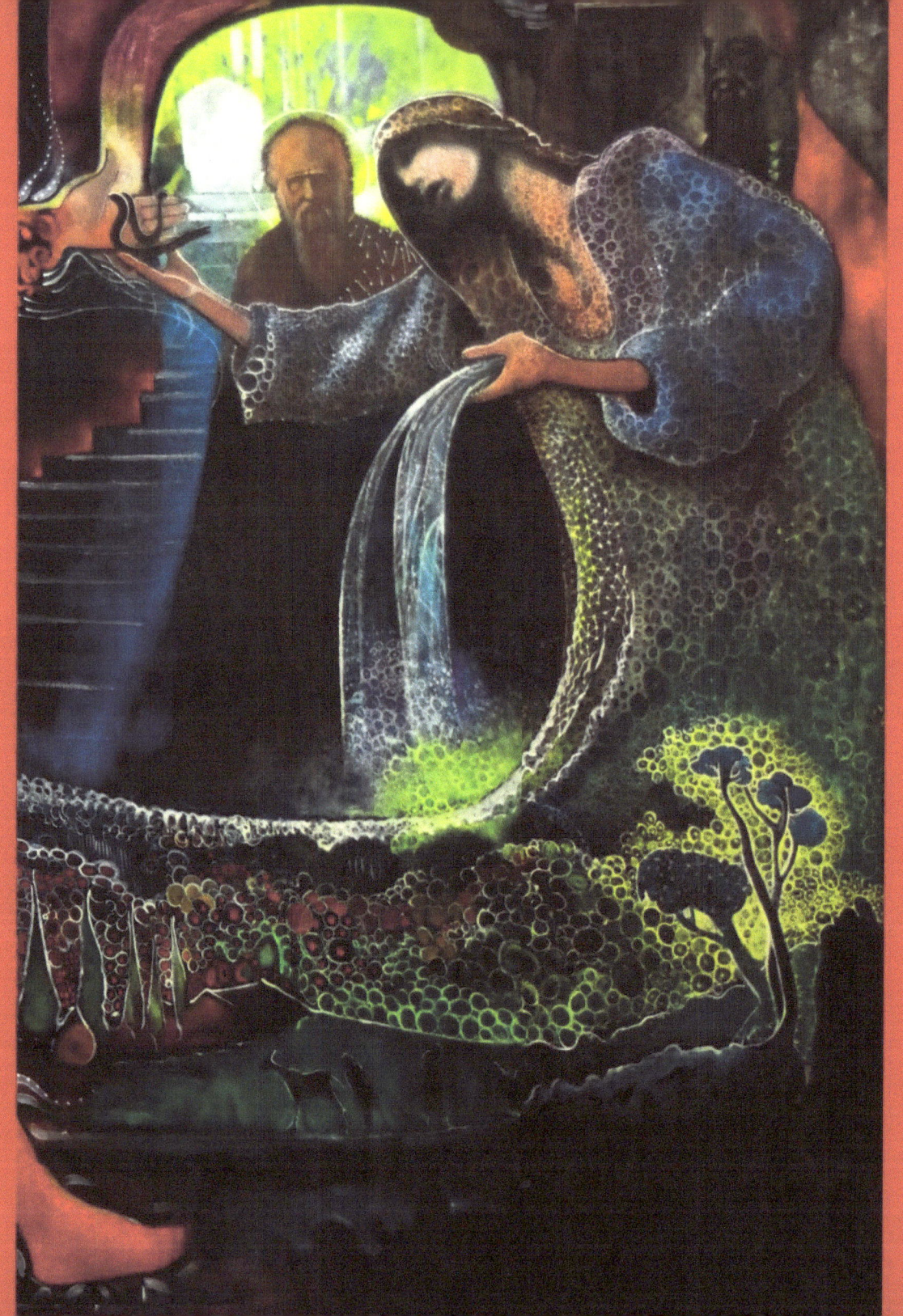

Beatrice

This part of the painting is still incomplete; most of the portraits have yet to be finished. Beatrice greets Dante and will become his guide (the painting also anticipates a future). Behind them are the angel stairs in Wells cathedral, and here waits Darwin and DaVinci, who will begin to introduce the great poet to all the new ideas that have emerged since he wended his way into the medieval hell..

The painting makes a romantic reference here, based on a photograph of a preraphaelite beauty.

The figure of Beatrice has been painted to emphasise her superabundance. She is personified superorganism, a great being made of beings.

Beatrice greets Dante. Behind is Mr Darwin waiting to be introduced

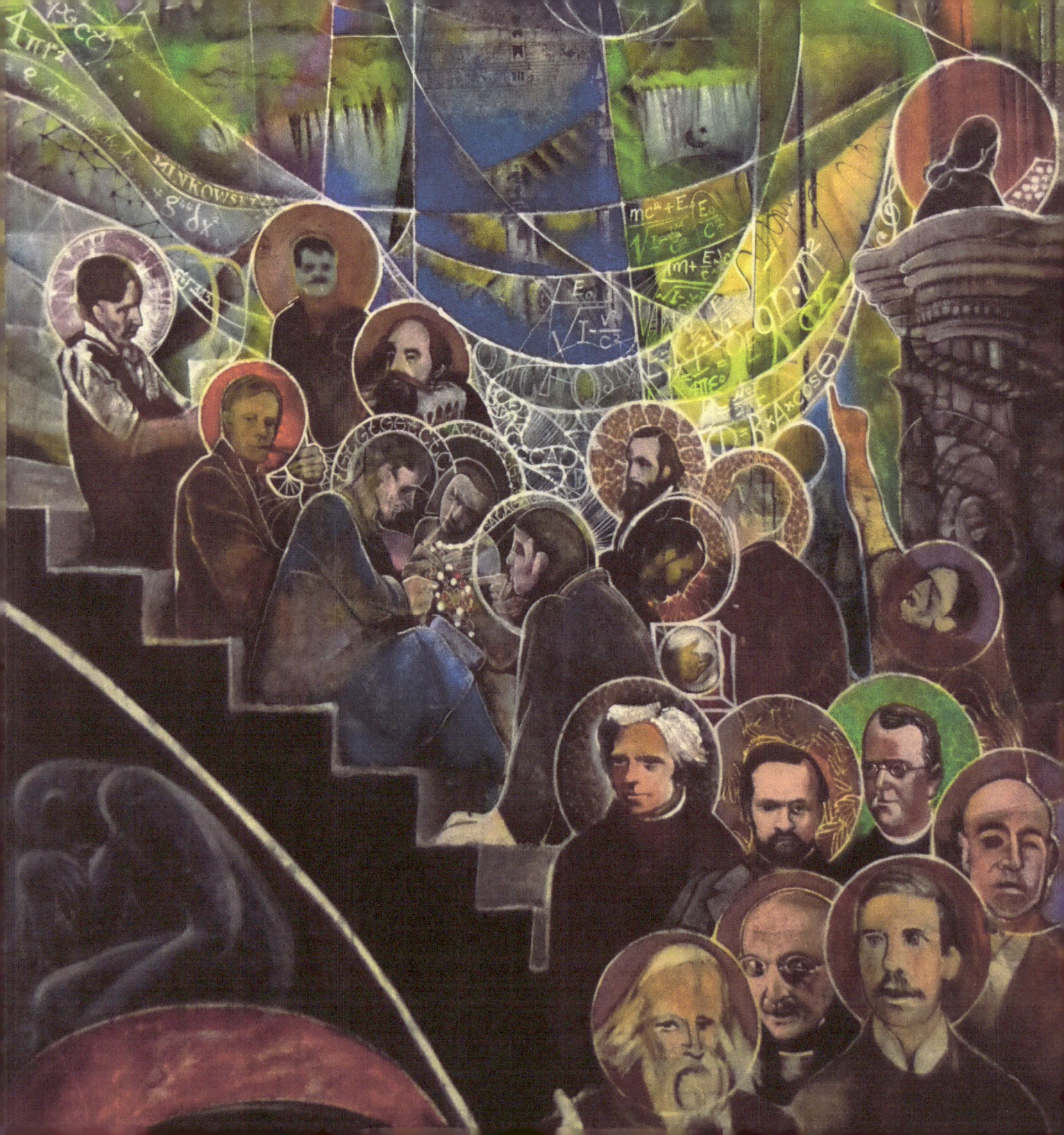

Verifiable Science

They will then proceed, the happy couple, up the staircase where a panoply of the great thinkers of our age are waiting. These are the men who have found a new way of cutting through the veils of mystery and ignorance, proceeding from the known to the unknown in minute segments of clarity, through verifiable science.

Here are Mendelev, Rutherford, Max Plank, Oppenheimer, Pasteur, Mendel, Feinmann, Bore, Fermi, Crick, Watson, Hubble (with a red shift) Maxwell, Malinovski are all waiting to meet the great poet.

The Great of science, who have made the discoveries that are examined in the wall painting. These men have based their discoveries on verifiable evidence, with peer review.

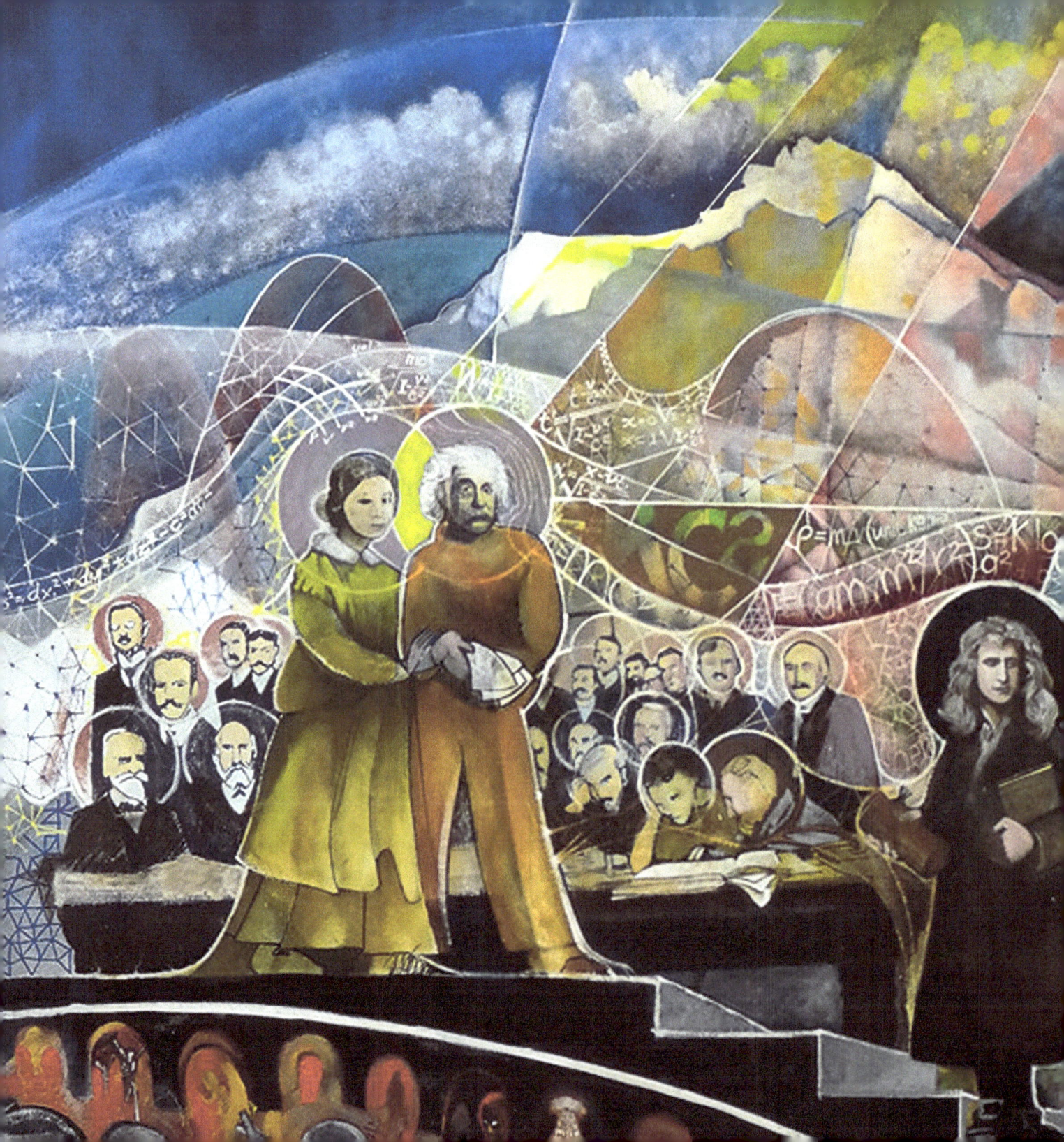

The Language of the Universe is written in Maths

Here stands Newton, holding his small telescope. Einstein and Mari Curi stand before the 1908 Solvai conference, a major moment in modern physics and astrophysics.

Between all these figures, embedded in a kind of matrix of waves and formulas are the mathematical equations by which these fellows have been able to describe the universe.

The language of the universe, as Newton said, is written in mathematics.

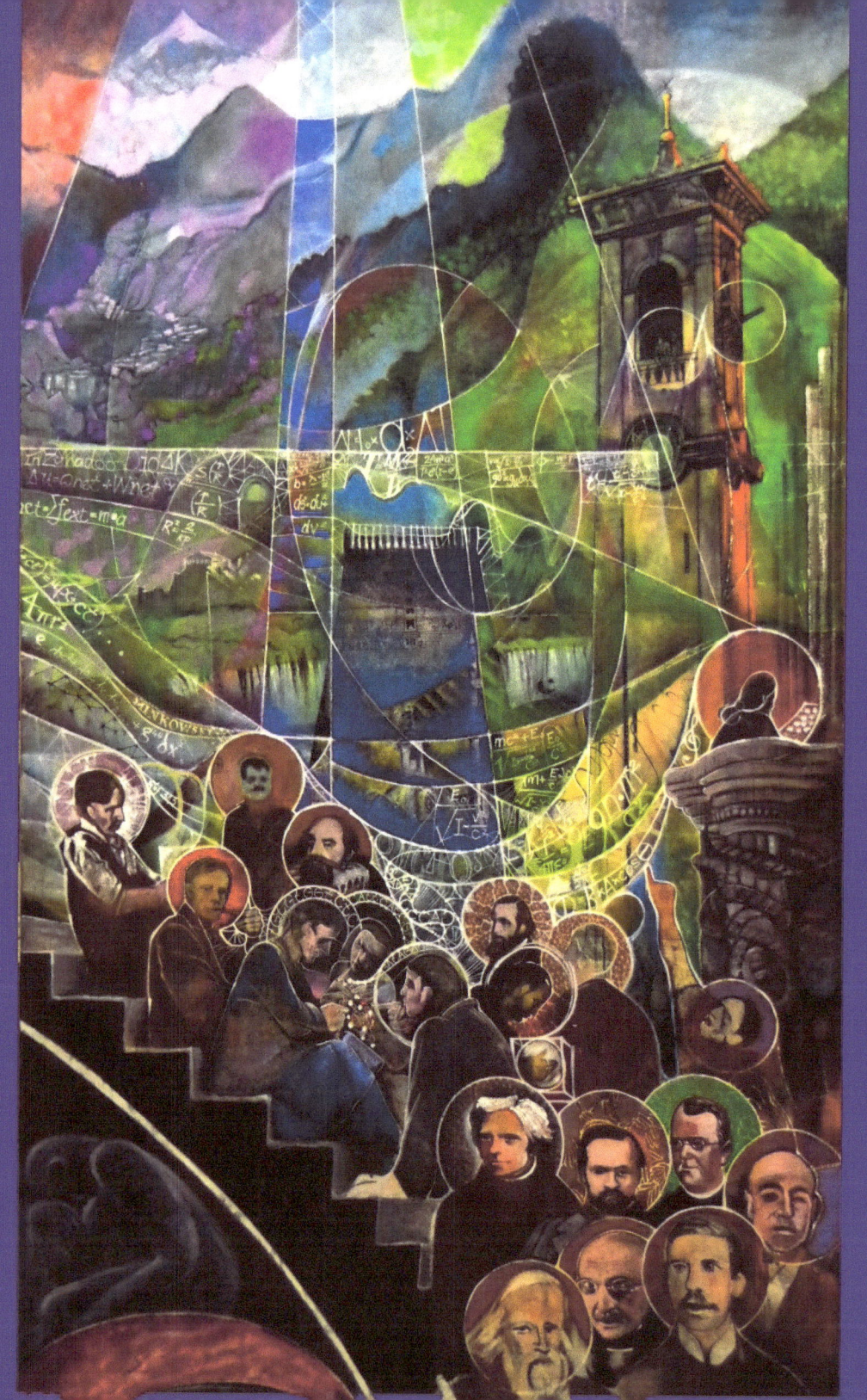

Verifiable Science II

Through this atmosphere can be glimpsed various images. The large Renaissance tower behind Bach is the site of some important experiments. If you look carefully you can see Copernicus mapping the moons of Jupiter and Galileo dropping his weights. 5th century Athens can be seen beyond a great chasm, where Plato's Academy is in session. Or maybe they could visit Socrates in his cell, before he chooses the hemlock.

The landscape above that was provoked by Coleridge's poem Kublai Khan.

At the top of the mountain, following an incredibly tortuous path, pausing maybe at a monastery to hear the dharma, they may visit one of the new observatories. They may be lucky enough to arrive at the very moment when we will observe for the first time, the moment just after the big bang. The better our telescopes become the further back in time we are able to see.

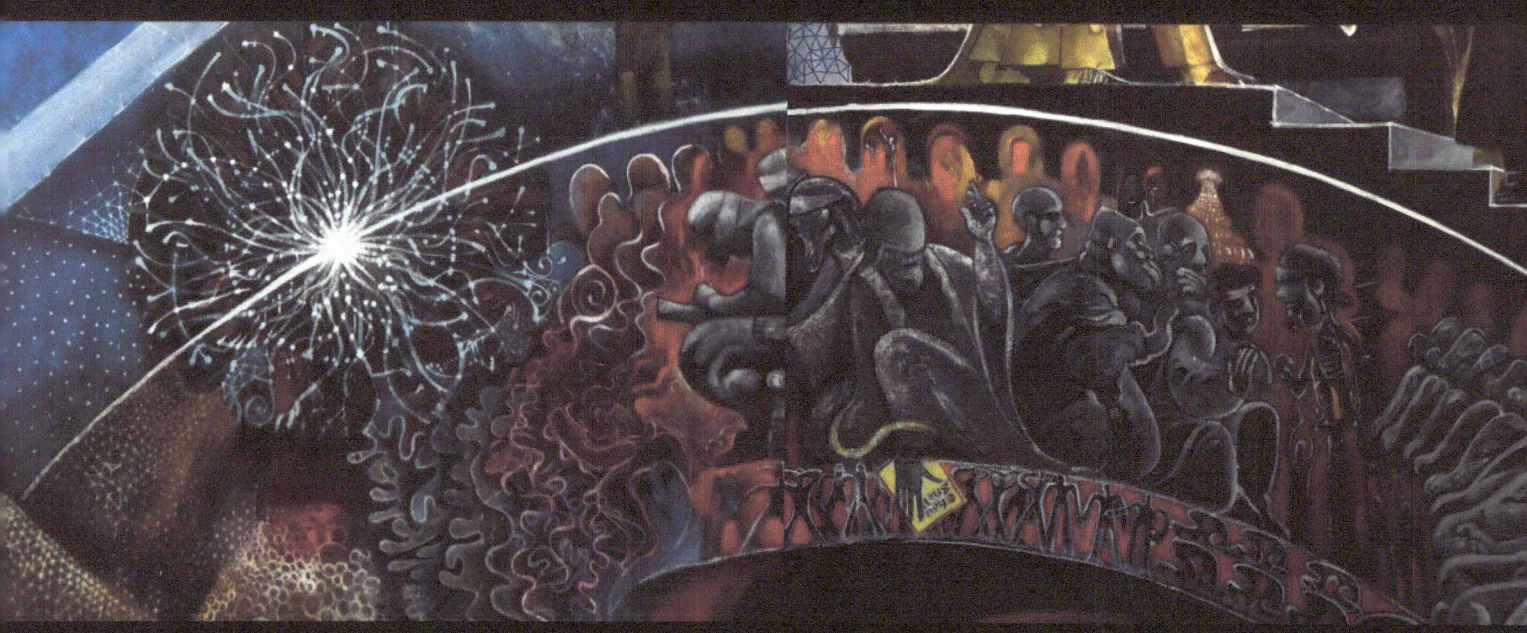

The Freize of the believers

The Believers

The edge of this arch and the frieze above makes reference to the human myth and cultures based on acceptance of old superstitious religions.

If you look carefully you can see the oracle of Delphi in the laurel smoke of the volcanic vent passing on her visions with a voice that sounded like the chattering of birds.

Here the blind are writing in books while other blind look on and St Simeon is still standing on his column.

Just above the believers, but under the mountain, is the GHC The Great Hadron Collider. Here cutting edge physics investigates the nature of our particulate universe.

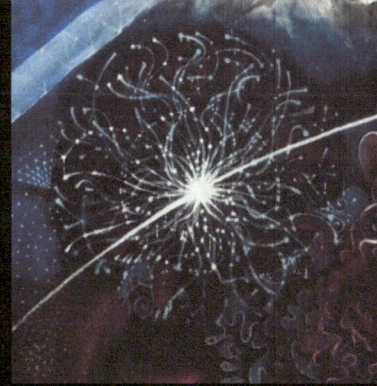

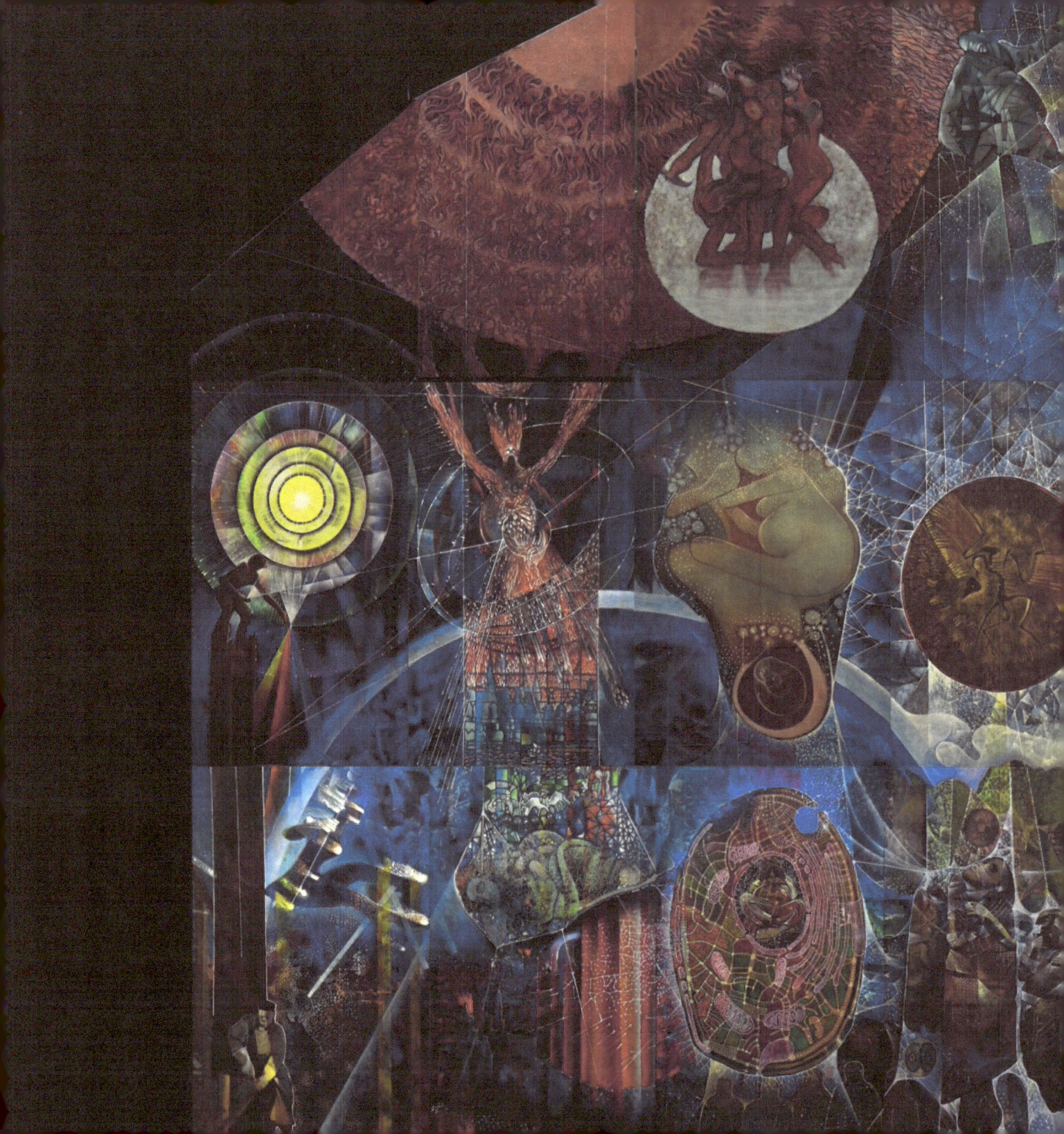

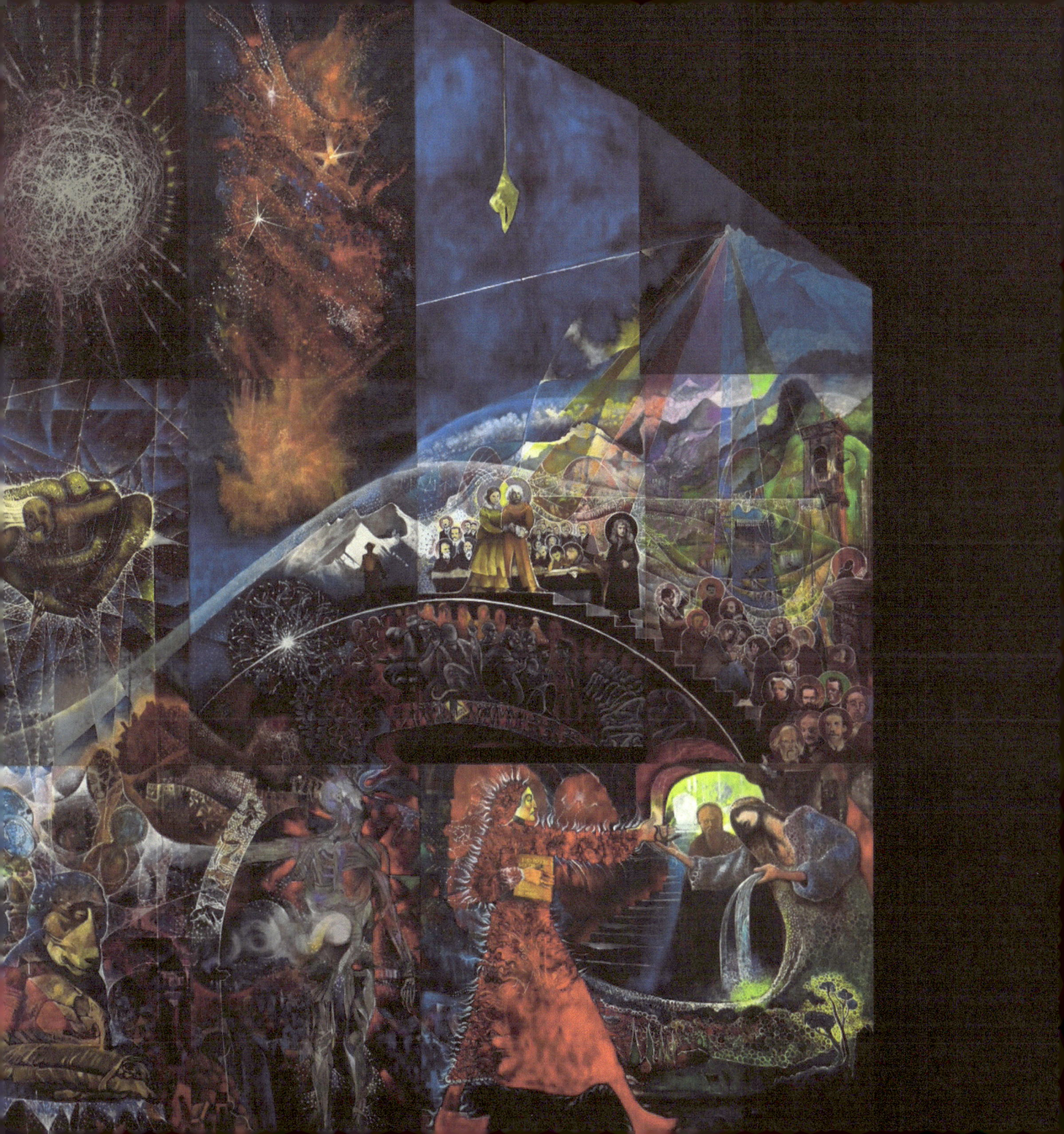

Published by

St John's Hall Gallery
St John's Road
Barmouth LL421AF

Tel: 07767862382

www.bernardbarnes.com

www.stjohnshallgallery.com

Synapticconnections@btopenworld.com

The author gratefully acknowledges

The help given by Karen Cropper in the

preparation of this text and Robbie Stocker

for photographing some of the images.

ISBN-13: 978-1515285069

ISBN-10: 1515285065

www.ingramcontent.com/pod-product-compliance
Lightning Source LLC
Chambersburg PA
CBHW050755180526
45159CB00003B/1472